Key Terms in Logic

Continuum *Key Terms in Philosophy*

The *Key Terms* series offers undergraduate students clear, concise and accessible introductions to core topics. Each book includes a comprehensive overview of the key terms, concepts, thinkers and texts in the area covered and ends with a guide to further resources.

Available now:

Key Terms in Philosophy of Mind, Pete Mandik
Key Terms in Philosophy of Religion, Raymond VanArragon

Key Terms in Philosophy forthcoming from Continuum:

Aesthetics, Brent Kalar
Ethics, Oskari Kuusela
Political Philosophy, Jethro Butler

Key Terms in Logic

Edited by Federica Russo and Jon Williamson

continuum

Continuum International Publishing Group
The Tower Building   80 Maiden Lane
11 York Road   Suite 704
London SE1 7NX   New York, NY 10038
www.continuumbooks.com

British Library Cataloguing-in-Publication Data
A catalogue record for this book is available from the British Library.

ISBN: HB: 978-1-8470-6113-3
        PB: 978-1-8470-6114-0

Library of Congress Cataloguing-in-Publication Data
Key terms in logic / edited by Federica Russo and Jon Williamson.
    p. cm.
Includes index.
ISBN: 978-1-8470-6113-3
        978-1-8470-6114-0
1. Logic. I. Williamson, Jon. II. Russo, Federica. III. Title.

BC108.K49 2010
160–dc22   2010005483

Typeset by Newgen Imaging Systems Pvt Ltd, Chennai, India
Printed and bound in India by Replika Press Pvt Ltd

Contents

List of Contributors

Andrew Aberdein [AA]
Department of Humanities and Communication, Florida Institute of Technology
aberdein@fit.edu

Robert Arp [RA]
OntoReason, McLean, VA
robertarp320@gmail.com

Conrad Asmus [CA]
The School of Philosophy, Anthropology and Social Inquiry, the University of Melbourne
conrad.asmus@gmail.com

Alan Baker [ABa]
Department of Philosophy, Swarthmore College
abaker1@swarthmore.edu

Michael Beaney [MB]
Department of Philosophy, University of York
mab505@york.ac.uk

Natan Berber [NB]
Department of Philosophy, University of Haifa
berber@research.haifa.ac.il

Katalin Bimbó [KB]
Department of Philosophy, University of Alberta
bimbo@ualberta.ca

Francesca Boccuni [FB]
Department of Philosophy, University of Padua
francesca.boccuni@tiscali.it

Ed Brandon [EB]
The Open Campus, the University of the West Indies, Barbados
edbrandon@gmail.com

Josephus Brimah [JB]
Department of Philosophy, Fourah Bay College, University of Sierra Leone
josephusbrimah@yahoo.co.uk

Alan Brown [ABr]
Independent scholar
entropy@hush.com

Elodie Cassan [EC]
CERPHI, France
ecassan@gmail.com

Gustavo Cevolani [GC]
Department of Philosophy, University of Bologna
g.cevolani@gmail.com

Leo K. C. Cheung [LC]
Department of Religion and Philosophy, Hong Kong Baptist University
kccheung@hkbu.edu.hk

Jean-Marie Chevalier [JMC]
Department of Philosophy, University of Paris-Est and Institut Jean Nicod
jeanmariechevalier@yahoo.fr

Benjamin Curtis [BC]
Department of Philosophy, University of Nottingham
ben.l.curtis@gmail.com

Kevin S. Decker [KD]
Department of Philosophy, Eastern Washington University
kdecker@mail.ewu.edu

Lieven Decock [LD]
Faculty of Philosophy, Vrije Universiteit Amsterdam
LB.Decock@ph.vu.nl

Ciro L. De Florio [CDF]
Department of Philosophy, Università cattolica di Milano
cirodeflorio@hotmail.com

Marcello Di Bello [MDB]
Department of Philosophy, Stanford University
marcello.dibello@gmail.com

Craig Fox [CF]
Department of Philosophy, California University of Pennsylvania
craig.d.fox@gmail.com

Henri Galinon [HG]
IHPST (CNRS / Université de Paris 1 / ENS)
henri.galinon@gmail.com

Jonathan Gillard [JG]
School of Mathematics, Cardiff University
gillardjw@cardiff.ac.uk

Donald Gillies [DG]
Department of Science and Technology Studies, University College London
donald.gillies@ucl.ac.uk

Norma B. Goethe [NBG]
School of Philosophy, National University of Cordoba
ngoethe@ffyh.unc.edu.ar

Laurence Goldstein [LG]
Department of Philosophy, University of Kent
l.goldstein@kent.ac.uk

Benoit Hardy-Vallée [BHV]
Department of Philosophy, University of Toronto
benoithv@gmail.com

Nigel Hee [NH]
Department of Philosophy, University of Glasgow
nigelhee@gmail.com

Conrad Heilmann [CH]
Department of Philosophy, Logic and Scientific Method, London School of
Economics and Political Science
C.Heilmann@lse.ac.uk

Matthew Hettche [MH]
Philosophy Department, Auburn University
hettcmr@auburn.edu

Amanda Hicks [AH]
Department of Philosophy, University at Buffalo
ahicks2@buffalo.edu

Dawn E. Holmes [DH]
Department of Statistics and Applied Probability, University of California,
Santa Barbara
holmes@pstat.ucsb.edu

Jean-Louis Hudry [JLH]
Department of Philosophy, University of Tartu
jl.hudry@gmail.com

Dale Jacquette [DJ]
Institute of Philosophy, Universtät Bern
dale.jacquette@philo.unibe.ch

Mark Jago [MJ]
Philosophy Department, Macquarie University
Mark.jago@scmp.mq.edu.au

Ludger Jansen [LJ]
Institute of Philosophy, University of Rostock
ludger.jansen@uni-rostock.de

Neil Kennedy [NK]
Department of Philosophy, University of Quebec in Montreal and Paris I
neil.patrick.kennedy@gmail.com

Morgan Luck [ML]
School of Humanities and Social Science, Charles Sturt University
moluck@csu.edu.au

Russell Marcus [RM]
Department of Philosophy, Hamilton College
rmarcus1@hamilton.edu

Casey McGinnis [CMG]
Department of Philosophy, University of Minnesota

Stephen McLeod [SML]
Department of Philosophy, University of Liverpool
Stephen.Mcleod@liverpool.ac.uk

Andrew P. Mills [APM]
Department of Religion and Philosophy, Otterbein College
AMills@otterbein.edu

Amirouche Moktefi [AM]
IRIST, Université de Strasbourg
LHSP Archives H. Poincaré, Nancy-Université
amirouche.moktefi@gersulp.u-strasbg.fr

Matteo Morganti [MMo]
Zukunftskolleg and Department of Philosophy, University of Konstanz
Matteo.Morganti@uni-konstanz.de

Julien Murzi [JM]
Philosophy Department, University of Sheffield
J.Murzi@sheffield.ac.uk

Mauro Murzi [MMu]
Member of the Società Filosofica Italiana
murzim@yahoo.com

Dan O'Brien [DOB]
Research Fellow, Oxford Brookes University
dan_obi@hotmail.com

Richard Pettigrew [RP]
Department of Philosophy, University of Bristol
Richard.Pettigrew@bristol.ac.uk

Francesca Poggiolesi [FP]
Center for Logic and Philosophy of Science (CLFW), Vrije Universiteit Brussel
and Logic Group of the University of Florence
poggiolesi@gmail.com

Jan-Willem Romeijn [JWR]
Philosophy, University of Groningen
j.w.romeijn@rug.nl

Constantine Sandis [CS]
Philosophy, Oxford Brookes University & New York University in London
csandis@brookes.ac.uk

Fabien Schang [FS]
LHSP Henri Poincaré, Nancy
Technische Universität Dresden, Institut für Philosophie
schang.fabien@voila.fr

Armin W. Schulz [AWS]
Department of Philosophy, Logic, and Scientific Method, London School of
Economics and Political Science
awschulz@wisc.edu

Marco Sgarbi [MS]
Dipartimento di Filosofia, Università di Verona
marco.sgarbi@lettere.univr.it

Hartley Slater [HS]
Philosophy, University of Western Australia
slaterbh@cyllene.uwa.edu.au

Rachel Sterken [RS]
Arché, University of St. Andrews

Apostolos Syropoulos [AS]
Independent scholar
asyropoulos@gmail.com

Sara L. Uckelman [SU]
Institute for Logic, Language & Computation, Universiteit van Amsterdam
S.L.Uckelman@uva.nl

Mark van Atten [MVA]
IHPST (CNRS / Université de Paris 1 / ENS)
Mark.vanAtten@univ-paris1.fr

Koen Vervloesem [KV]
Independent scholar
koen@vervloesem.eu

Zach Weber [ZW]
Sydney Centre for the Foundations of Science, School of Philosophical and
Historical Inquiry, University of Sydney
School of Philosophy and Social Inquiry, University of Melbourne
zach.weber@usyd.edu.au

John N. Williams [JW]
School of Social Sciences, Singapore Management University
johnwilliams@smu.edu.sg

Frank Zenker [FZ]
Department of Philosophy and Cognitive Science, Lund University
frank.zenker@fil.lu.se

List of Symbols

Symbol	Description	How to Read it	Example
wff	Abbreviation of 'well formed formula', i.e. any string of symbols within the vocabulary of a language L that obeys the rules (syntax) of L	Well-formed formula	'It is sunny' in English $A \cup B$ in set theory $(P \to Q)$ in propositional logic etc.
iff	Abbreviation of 'if and only if'	If and only if	$P \leftrightarrow Q$ The moon is made of blue cheese if and only if pigs can fly
P, Q, R	Propositional letters / variables	[pronounce the letter]	P The moon is made of blue cheese
$\Phi, \psi, \chi,$ A, B, C	Propositions / wffs / statements	[pronounce the letter]	Any proposition
$\neg$	Negation	not P it is not the case that P	$\neg P$ The moon is not made of blue cheese
$\to$	Implication / material conditional	If P then Q P implies Q	$P \to Q$ If the moon is made of blue cheese, pigs can fly
$\leftrightarrow$	Double implication / biconditional	P if and only if Q	$P \leftrightarrow Q$ The moon is made of blue cheese if and only if pigs can fly

∧	Conjunction	*P* and *Q*	*P* ∧ *Q* The moon is made of blue cheese and pigs can fly
∨	Disjunction	*P* or *Q*	*P* ∨ *Q* The moon is made of blue cheese or pigs can fly
x, y	Individual variables	[pronounce the letter]	*x* Any element of a set (the domain)
a, b, c	Individual constants	[pronounce the letter]	*a* The moon
F, G	Predicate symbols	[pronounce the letter]	Is made of blue cheese
Fa		[pronounce the letters]	*Fa* The moon is made of blue cheese
∀	Universal quantifier	For all *x*	∀*xFx* All elements of the domain are made of blue cheese
∃	Existential quantifier	There exists an *x* such that . . .	∃*xFx* At least one element of the domain is made of blue cheese
◊	Modal operator of possibility	It is possible that *P* In some possible world it is true that *P*	◊*P* It is possible that the moon is made of blue cheese
☐	Modal operator of necessity	It is necessary that *P* In every possible world it is true that *P*	☐*P* It is necessary that the moon is made of blue cheese

(Continued)

Symbol	Description	How to Read it	Example
≡	Logical equivalence	P is logically equivalent to Q	$P \equiv P \wedge P$ The proposition that the moon is made of blue cheese is logically equivalent to the proposition that the moon is made of blue cheese and the moon is made of blue cheese
∴	Therefore	P. Therefore, Q.	$P \therefore Q$ The moon is made of blue cheese. Therefore, pigs can fly
⊢	Syntactic consequence relation	Q is a syntactic consequence of P.	$P \vdash Q$ That pigs can fly is a syntactic consequence of the moon being made of blue cheese
⊨	Semantic entailment relation	P logically implies Q	$P \vDash Q$ The moon being made of blue cheese logically implies that pigs can fly
≥	Greater than or equal to	[a] is greater or equal to [b]	$a \geq b$ Jon's age is greater than or equal to Federica's age
≤	Less than or equal to	[a] is less than or equal to [b]	$a \leq b$ Jon's age is less than or equal to Federica's age

$A = \{a, b, c, ...\}$	Representation of a set	Set A has as elements a, b, c.	$A = \{1, 2, 3\}$: the set A has as elements 1, 2 and 3
$A = \{x \in B \mid f(x)\}$		Set A has as elements the elements x of B that have the property f	$A = \{n \in N \mid n \leq 3\}$: the set A has as elements all the natural numbers less than or equal to 3
U	The universe / domain of discourse	The universe of discourse	The set of all the elements under consideration
$\varnothing$	The empty set	Empty set	Any set that has no elements in it
$\in$	Relation of membership	$a \in A$ element a belongs to the set A	$a \in A$ Jon belongs to the set of philosophers of the University of Kent
$\notin$	Negated relation of membership	$a \notin A$ element a does not belong to the set A	$a \notin A$ Federica does not belong the set of secretaries of the University of Kent
$\cap$	Intersection	$A \cap B$ A intersected with B	If $A = \{1, 3, 5\}$ and $B = \{1, 2, 4\}$ then $A \cap B = \{1\}$
$\cup$	Union	$A \cup B$ A united with B	If $A = \{1, 3, 5\}$ and $B = \{1, 2, 4\}$ then $A \cup B = \{1, 2, 3, 4, 5\}$
$\subset$	Inclusion, or proper subset	$A \subset B$ A is a proper subset of B [or] A is included in B	The set A of logicians is a proper subset of the set B of philosophers at the University of Kent

(Continued)

Symbol	Description	How to Read it	Example
$\subseteq$	Inclusion, or subsubset	$A \subseteq B$ A is a subset of B [or] A is a proper subset of, or is identical to B	The set A of logicians at the University of Kent is a subset of the set B of the philosophers at the University of Kent. [supposing that all the logicians are philosophers]
$P(E)$	Probability of E	The probability of E	E = head at a coin toss $P(E) = \frac{1}{2}$
$P(E\mid F)$	Probability of E conditional on F $P(E\mid F) = \dfrac{P(E \cap F)}{P(F)}$	The probability of E given F	E = pick a heart card from a deck of 52 cards F = a heart card has already been taken from the same deck $P(E\mid F)$ = 12/51

Introduction

This volume sets out to provide a reference for students starting out in philosophy, as well as those in other disciplines – such as computing, mathematics, psychology and law – in which logic features prominently.

Logic can be thought of in a variety of ways. It is sometimes viewed as the study of consistency, concerned with asking when statements are consistent and when they are inconsistent. But logic is more often conceived of as the study of consequence – what follows from what. Thus deductive logic studies valid consequence (situations in which the truth of the premises of an argument forces the truth of its conclusion) while inductive logic studies plausible or probable consequence (situations in which the premises render the conclusion more probable or sufficiently probable). Important goals of logic include characterizing interesting consequence relationships (e.g., deductive consequence, inductive consequence) and providing practical methods for answering questions about these consequence relationships (e.g., truth tables, semantic trees and proof are three ways of determining whether a conclusion follows from given premises in deductive logic).

Logic is sometimes held to be the theory of reasoning. While it certainly teaches us a lot about how we can and ought to reason, logics are occasionally applied to tasks that do not obviously concern reasoning, such as to the modelling of hardware in computer science, and so some philosophers view logic and reasoning as somewhat different. Logic is often also distinguished from decision-making: logic is thought to be about theoretical relationships between statements while decision-making is apparently guided by pragmatic considerations such as the utilities or values attached to actions. On the other hand, logics (in particular inductive logics) are sometimes justified by appealing to pragmatic goals such as the goal of minimizing loss and it is clear that the relationship between logic and decision-making is rather subtle.

There is no need to decide these subtle questions in order to study and enjoy logic – at the very least, logic studies consequence and this is enough to make logic crucial to philosophy and to other disciplines concerned with cogent argument. But bewildering terminology can delay the study and enjoyment of logic; it is hoped that this volume will help the reader to understand some of the key jargon. The volume is organized in three parts: Key Terms, Key Thinkers and Key Texts (divided into Textbooks and Classics). Entries are arranged alphabetically in each part and a list of symbols used in the book is in the front of the volume.

The volume is a collaborative effort, with entries provided by a multitude of authors. Each entry is initialled and the authors are listed in the front of the volume. We are very grateful to the authors for all the hard work they have put into the volume and for contributing many of the entries to *The Reasoner* (www.thereasoner.org). We are particularly grateful to Amirouche Moktefi, Francesca Boccuni, Ed Brandon and Laurence Goldstein for many suggestions of improvements to the text.

Key Terms

A Priori / A Posteriori. A proposition is knowable a priori if one can know that it is true without appeal to experience. In order to know that bachelors are unmarried men I do not have to interview various bachelors; I just have to understand the terms 'bachelor' and 'unmarried man'. In contrast, a proposition is knowable a posteriori if it can be known on the basis of experience. That sugar is sweet is knowable a posteriori because I can come to know this by tasting it. *See also* ANALYTIC-SYNTHETIC; NECESSITY; KRIPKE, SAUL; MILL, JOHN STUART. [DOB]

Abduction. Abduction is a nonmonotonic pattern of reasoning involved both in hypothesis formulation and explanation. While deduction determines necessary consequences and induction determines probable ones, abductive reasoning determines which plausible hypothesis would make sense of an already observed consequence. Abduction is also referred to as inference to the best explanation, that is, concluding that one explanation is true from the fact that it provides a better explanation than any other. Although it is defeasible (compelling but not deductively valid), abduction has an important role in scientific discovery and artificial intelligence. *See also* ANALOGY; BELIEF REVISION; CONDITION, NECESSARY AND SUFFICIENT; CONSEQUENT; DEDUCTION; INDUCTION; PROBABILITY; INFERENCE TO THE BEST EXPLANATION; LOGIC, NONMONOTONIC; SOUNDNESS. [BHV]

Absorption. *See* INFERENCE, RULES OF.

Abstraction. Traditionally, abstraction indicates a process of derivation of a universal from the particulars that fall under it. In second- and higher order logics, abstraction is expressed by the Axiom of Comprehension $\exists P \forall x \, (Px \equiv \varphi)$, which states the existence of a property or class P for every formula φ of the language. The principle of λ-Conversion $\forall y \, [\lambda x.Px](y) \equiv \varphi \, (y/x)$, where $[\lambda x.Px]$ might be read as 'the property P', is also an abstraction principle according to which every individual *y* falls under the property *P* if and only if *y* satisfies φ. Set theory displays a similar axiom, $\exists \alpha \forall x$ ($x \in \alpha \equiv \varphi$), which says that there is a set α of all *x* such that φ holds. *See also* AXIOM; CLASSES; PROPERTY; SET THEORY; TYPE THEORY. [FB]

Analogy. An analogy is a logical function and a reasoning process. As a logical function, analogy is a relation between two ordered pairs: in '*A* is to *B* as *C* is to *D*', the particular elements are different but the functional relation is identical. As a reasoning process, an analogy is a structure-preserving mapping between two conceptual domains: a 'source' and a 'target', the first one being familiar, the second unfamiliar. Properties of items in the source domain are applied to items in the target domain. Analogy is thought to be important in abduction. *See also* ABDUCTION; DOMAIN; INFERENCE; INFERENCE TO THE BEST EXPLANATION; INDUCTION; LOGIC, NONMONOTONIC; LOGICAL FUNCTION. [BHV]

Addition. *See* INFERENCE, RULES OF.

AGM. AGM is the paradigmatic approach to belief revision named after C.E. Alchourrón, P. Gärdenfors, D. Makinson (1985. On the logic of theory change: partial meet contraction and revision functions. *Journal of Symbolic Logic*, 50: 510–30). AGM axiomatically models the change of a fully believed, consistent and deductively closed set of sentences (aka theory), *K*, in response to new information, *p*, which is inconsistent with the set. An entrenchment order, $\leq$, specifies which sentences are to be retracted from the belief set when an inconsistency is found. *See also* BELIEF REVISION; LOGIC, DYNAMIC; LOGIC, NONMONOTONIC; SET; SET THEORY; THEORY. [FZ]

Analytic / Synthetic. Analytic propositions are true by definition; their truth follows from the meanings of the terms used to express such propositions. Thus 'Pain hurts' is analytic. The truth of synthetic propositions, however, depends on more than the meanings of their constituent terms. That 'Henry is fat' does not follow from merely the meaning of 'Henry', 'is' and 'fat'; this is therefore a synthetic truth. Note that the analytic / synthetic distinction differs from that concerning the a priori / a posteriori; the former distinction is semantic (concerning meaning), whereas the latter is epistemological (concerning the acquisition of knowledge). Much philosophy has focused on whether there are any synthetic a priori propositions. *See also* A PRIORI / A POSTERIORI; LOGICISM; NECESSITY; QUINE, WILLARD VAN ORMAN. [DOB]

Antecedent. One of two logical parts of a conditional statement, often preceded by 'if'. Consider: 'If lamb is prepared tonight, I'll eat'; the antecedent is 'lamb is prepared tonight'. Whatever plays this logical role is the antecedent. *See also* CONDITIONAL; CONSEQUENT; MATERIAL IMPLICATION. [CF]

Antinomy. A pair of contradictory propositions, each of which can be demonstrated using a valid deductive proof, thereby giving rise to a contradiction or paradox. Paradigmatic examples appear in law and jurisprudence, where two legal judgments, standing as mutually exclusive and mutually exhaustive alternatives, are both justified by the same law (or set of laws). As a philosophical term, 'antinomy' receives perhaps its most extensive development in the critical works of Kant. In the Critique of Pure Reason, for example, Kant outlines four 'cosmological antinomies' that deal with the structure of the universe (or world-whole), the divisibility of matter, causality and the existence of God. According to Kant, the 'dialectical opposition' between the 'thesis' and 'antithesis' of these antinomies results from reason's attempt to transcend the limits of possible experience. Other German Idealists, such as Fichte and Hegel, also develop the term in a philosophical sense. More recently, however, in the works of twentieth century analytic philosophers, such as Russell, Ramsey and Quine, the term 'antinomy' is more narrowly applied to problems of logic and mathematics (including, but not limited to, paradoxes of infinity and paradoxes involving part–whole relationships). *See also* CONTRADICTION; DEDUCTION; PARADOXES; VALIDITY; RUSSELL, BERTRAND; QUINE, WILLARD VAN ORMAN. [MH]

Argument. An argument is a connected series of propositions, of which exactly one is the conclusion and the rest are premises, or steps on the way from premises to the conclusion. There are two major categories of arguments. In deductive arguments, the premises are intended to force the truth of the conclusion. In inductive arguments, the premises are intended to raise the likelihood, or probability, of the conclusion. In evaluating arguments, we may examine both the truth of the premises and the ways in which the premises work together to establish the truth (or likelihood) of the conclusion; the latter question is the focus of logicians. *See also* CONCLUSION; DEDUCTION; INDUCTION; PREMISS; PROBABILITY; PROPOSITION; SOUNDNESS; VALIDITY. [APM]

Argumentation Theory. Argumentation theory is the study of argument, particularly those aspects which resist deductive formalization. It is often taken to coincide with or subsume informal logic and critical thinking.

Aristotle's *Organon*, famous as the first study of formal logic, actually pays greater attention to informal reasoning. Notably, Aristotle introduces 'enthymemes', latterly over-simplified as syllogisms with missing premisses, to characterize plausible non-deductive inferences. Logic retained this broader scope into the early twentieth century, until the increasingly successful mathematical approach eclipsed all others.

The modern revival of argumentation theory began with two works: Chaim Perelman and Lucie Olbrechts-Tyteca's *La Nouvelle Rhétorique* (1958. Paris: Presses Universitaires de France) and Stephen Toulmin's *The Uses Of Argument* (1958. Cambridge: Cambridge University Press). Both emphasize jurisprudential over mathematical approaches to reasoning. Toulmin's major contribution was the 'layout' which analyses arguments into six components. The data (or grounds) provide qualified support for the claim in accordance with a warrant, which may in turn be supported by backing or admit exceptions or rebuttals.

Toulmin's influence was greatest outside philosophy, and recent work is strongly interdisciplinary, encompassing communication theory, artificial intelligence and law. For instance, 'pragma-dialectics', the influential pro-gramme of Amsterdam communication theorists Frans van Eemeren and Rob Grootendorst, advocates a normative ideal for critical discussion. This is characterized by 'Ten Commandments': rules claimed to be necessary for a reasonable outcome in a disagreement. Conversely, some artificial intelligence research connects argumentation to formal accounts of defeasible reasoning, such as nonmonotonic logic.

Much recent attention has focused on 'argumentation schemes': stereotypical patterns of plausible reasoning. These may be seen as reinventing Aristotle's 'topoi', which linked the premisses to the conclusion in his enthymemes. Argumentation schemes are important to the long-standing problem of characterizing informal fallacies. Fallacies may be understood as pathological instances of plausible but not invariably sound schemes. This programme has been developed at length by the logician Douglas Walton. *See also* ARGUMENT; FALLACY; LOGIC, NONMONOTONIC; SYLLOGISM; ORGANON. [AA]

Assumption. A proposition which is taken for granted in a proof. The truth of the assumption may be ascertained in a separate proof. If, however, a contradiction can be inferred from an unproven assumption, this proves that the assumption is false. Such a proof is called a proof by contradiction. *See also* CONTRADICTION; HYPOTHESIS; PROOF; PROPOSITION. [KV]

Axiom. An axiom is a proposition which is considered fundamental. Epistemically, axioms are considered as self-evident truths. Derivationally, they are essential in that all the theorems of a theory can be derived from them.

In axiomatic theories, *logical axioms* are the fundamental propositions that display the logical content of a theory (for instance, the Principle of the Excluded Middle). *Non-logical axioms* are the basic propositions that concern the substantive content of a theory (in usual axiomatic theories for arithmetic, for instance, the axiom that states that 0 is the successor of no number is a non-logical axiom). *See also* EXCLUDED MIDDLE, PRINCIPLE OF; PROPOSITION; THEOREM. [FB]

Barcan Formulae. The Barcan formula, first studied by Ruth Barcan Marcus, states: $\Diamond(\exists x)F(x)\rightarrow(\exists x)\Diamond F(x)$, or in words: 'If it's possible that there exists an x for which F holds, then there exists an x for which it's possible that F holds.' The converse Barcan formula is: $(\exists x)\Diamond F(x)\rightarrow\Diamond(\exists x)F(x)$, or in words: 'If there exists an x for which it's possible that F holds, it is possible that there exists an x for which F holds.' Intuitively speaking, the Barcan formula states that nothing comes into existence when moving from a possible world to an alternative world. The converse Barcan formula states that nothing goes out of existence. Taken together, they say that the domain of quantification stays fixed in all possible worlds. *See also* DOMAIN; EXISTENTIAL QUANTIFIER; LOGIC, MODAL; POSSIBLE WORLD; QUANTIFIER. [KV]

Bayes' Theorem. Let A and B be events; for example, suppose A is the event 'x tested positive on pregnancy test t' and B is the event 'x is pregnant'. Bayes' theorem allows us to calculate the probability of B given A – the probability that x is pregnant given that t is positive – assuming the probabilities of A, B and A given B, as follows: $P(B|A) = P(B)P(A|B)/P(A)$. The posterior probability of B is the prior probability of B times an 'updating factor' $P(A|B)/P(A)$. Suppose $P(A) = 0.2$, $P(B) = 0.15$ and $P(A|B)$, the probability of testing positive if pregnant, is 0.95, then $P(B|A) = P(B)P(A|B)/P(A) = 0.15*0.95/0.2 = 0.7125$. *See also* BAYESIANISM; PROBABILITY; PROBABILITY, INTERPRETATION OF. [NK]

Bayesianism. A viewpoint originating in the work of Thomas Bayes (but mostly developed in the twentieth century) stressing the usefulness of probabilistic reasoning in settling many debates in philosophy and in the sciences. It is often characterized by a commitment to two theses: (1) probabilities represent (rational) degrees of belief; (2) degrees of belief are rationally revised according to Bayes' theorem (they are 'conditionalized') – an agent's beliefs after she has learned something new should be equal to her old beliefs, conditional on the newly acquired fact. Through (1) and (2), Bayesians seek to develop a formal apparatus that sharpens various complex debates, and thereby makes them theoretically tractable.

Important areas that Bayesianism has been applied to include the philosophy of science, statistics, logic and cognitive science. In the philosophy of science, Bayesianism has mostly been used to explain when a theory is empirically confirmed: this is said to happen when the evidence leads scientists to (rationally) increase their degree of belief in the theory being true. Other applications of the account comprise improvements in the testing of statistical hypotheses, extensions of traditional logic into the realm of beliefs and models of actual thought processes.

However, the account is not without its critics. First, some argue that it gets many important facts wrong: that numerous instances of scientific confirmation, hypothesis testing and ordinary thought do not seem to be captured well by Bayesian models. Secondly, some critics are worried about the key role that beliefs play in the theory: they think that science and logic are concerned with objective relationships among facts and propositions, not with beliefs (rational or otherwise). Despite these worries, though, Bayesianism is currently the dominant theory of confirmation in the philosophy of science, and also of considerable importance in many other areas of science. *See also* BAYES' THEOREM; LOGIC, PROBABILISTIC; PROBABILITY; PROBABILITY, INTERPRETATION OF; PROPOSITION; BAYES, THOMAS; JEFFREY, RICHARD. [AWS]

Belief Revision. In a broad sense, belief revision is synonymous with belief change; in a narrow sense, it is a specific type of belief change. For belief change comes in three forms: expansion, contraction and revision (in the narrow sense). Expansion is the addition of a new belief to the agent's current set of beliefs. Contraction, instead, is the removal of existing beliefs from the agent's set of beliefs. Finally, revision takes place when the addition of a new belief to the agent's set of beliefs would cause the resulting set to be inconsistent. To preserve consistency, agents can either reject the new belief, or accept it and accordingly adjust the resulting belief set such that inconsistencies are avoided. The latter option is revision.

While expansion can be formalized by simple set-theoretic union, contraction and revision are harder to formalize. The difficulty with contraction is that if a belief is removed and if the removed belief is entailed by other beliefs, some of the entailing beliefs must be removed as well. The difficulty with revision is to find a way of preserving consistency. To illustrate, suppose a child holds the following beliefs:

(1) All big-sized animals living in the water are fish.
(2) Fish are not mammals.

While seeing a whale living in the ocean, the child concludes:

(3) Whales are big-sized animals living in the water; hence by (1) and (2)
(4) Whales are not mammals.

Beliefs (1), (2), (3) and (4) constitute the child's belief set. Later in school, the teacher tells the child that (4) is unwarranted. As the teacher is a reliable source, the child must remove (4) from her set of beliefs. But (4) follows from (1), (2) and (3), so the child must remove at least one of them. Deciding which belief to remove and designing a general procedure to do so is a non-trivial question.

A similar problem arises for revision. Given the child's beliefs consisting of (1), (2), (3) and (4), suppose the teacher tells the child:

(5) Whales are mammals.

The child trusts the teacher, so she accepts (5), which however conflicts with (4). So the child must give up (4), but as seen for contraction, the task of giving up (4) is non-trivial. In order to provide a general procedure for revision or contraction, one strategy is to define rationality postulates with which any rational agent is thought to comply. The first instance of this strategy is encompassed by what are called the AGM postulates. Two subsequent contributions are worth mentioning: Grove (1988. Two modellings for theory change. *Journal of Philosophical Logic*, 17: 157–70) in which belief revision is linked to counterfactual reasoning; and Segerberg (1998. Irrevocable belief revision in dynamic doxastic logic. *Notre Dame Journal of Formal Logic*, 39: 287–306) in which a logic for belief revision with proof-system, semantics and completeness results is provided. *See also* AGM; IMPLICATION; LOGIC, DYNAMIC. [MDB and RS]

Biconditional. The biconditional (symbol: $\leftrightarrow$) is one of the sixteen truth-functional connectives in classical propositional logic. For any variables A and B, $A \leftrightarrow B$ is true whenever A and B have the same truth-value. The biconditional can also be defined as the conjunction of two conditionals: $A \leftrightarrow B$ can be defined as $(A \rightarrow B) \wedge (B \rightarrow A)$. The biconditional should be distinguished from equivalence: equivalence is a valid biconditional, that is, true under every interpretation of its components. Therefore, A and B are equivalent whenever they have the same truth-value under every interpretation.

The same distinction obtains between the conditional and logical implication. *See also* CONDITION, NECESSARY AND SUFFICIENT; MATERIAL EQUIVALENCE. [FS]

Binary. Binary can refer to a two-place relation between two individuals ('loves' in 'John loves Mary' is a binary relation between 'John' and 'Mary'), or a variable which takes one of two values such as 1 or 0, or True or False. Other examples of binary relations are 'taller than' and 'greater than'. *See also* BOOLEAN; VARIABLE. [NH]

Bivalence. The principle of bivalence claims that every proposition has exactly one of two possible truth-values: true or false. Though widely accepted, some claim the existence of a third truth-value and so deny bivalence. Candidate propositions that may have this third value are those whose singular terms fail to refer, for example, 'The Prime Minister of the USA is wise' and those propositions for which confirming or refuting evidence is in principle unavailable, for example, 'Sophie was charitable' said of a person, now dead, who never encountered a situation that required her to manifest either her charity or her miserliness. *See also* BROUWER'S PROGRAMME; EXCLUDED MIDDLE, PRINCIPLE OF; INTUITIONISM; TRUTH-VALUE. [APM]

Boolean. George Boole reinterpreted categorical propositions as relations between classes. He devised a binary system (known as 'Boolean logic') whose elements are assigned one of two possible values – either '1' or '0'.

In its basics, Boolean logic uses one unary operator, logical NOT, and two binary operators, logical OR and AND. These correspond to '$\neg$', '$\vee$' and '$\wedge$'. Applying these operators to the possible values of A and B, we obtain the following truth-table:

A	B	$A \vee B$	$A \wedge B$	$\neg A$
1	1	1	1	0
1	0	1	0	0
0	1	1	0	1
0	0	0	0	1

From these, we can derive other operations, such as Boolean equality, material implication and exclusive OR.

Boolean equality:	$(A \equiv B) = \neg(A \oplus B)$
Material implication:	$(A \rightarrow B) = \neg(A \wedge \neg B)$
Exclusive OR:	$(A \oplus B) = (A \vee B) \wedge \neg(A \wedge B)$

Boolean logic bears many similarities to propositional logic, including but not limited to: the laws of associativity, commutativity, absorption, distributivity, idempotency and being finitely axiomatizable. Every Boolean term (expressions built up using variables, the constants 1 and 0 and the basic operators) has a corresponding propositional formula – Boolean variables become propositional variables, 1 and 0 become 'true' and 'false', respectively. This is because propositional logic is interpreted truth-functionally. Boolean logic is also reflexive $(A = A)$, transitive $(A = B = C) = (A = C)$, symmetrical $(A = B) = (B = A)$ and substitutive (if $A = B \vee C$ then $\vdash \neg A \wedge D = \neg(B \vee C) \wedge D$). Boolean logic is both sound and complete.

Being a two-valued logic, Boolean logic is used in computer programming, mathematical logic, set theory and statistics, among other fields and areas. For example, the Boolean logic lends itself perfectly to computer programmers coding in assembly language or other low-level languages, where lines of code are broken down into binary operations. *See also* BINARY; CLASSES; COMPLETENESS; CATEGORICAL PROPOSITION; LOGIC, PROPOSITIONAL; LOGICAL OPERATOR; SOUNDNESS; TRUTH-FUNCTIONAL; TRUTH-TABLE; BOOLE, GEORGE. [NH]

Brouwer's Programme. Brouwer's programme, which he called 'Intuitionism', aims to provide a philosophical foundation for pure mathematics. The idea is that mathematics is first of all the activity of making exact constructions in the mind. The material out of which these constructions are made is abstracted from the intuition of the flow of time in consciousness. Accordingly, there is no mathematical reality outside the mind, and with every new construction not only our mathematical knowledge, but the mathematical universe itself grows. Brouwer sharply distinguished Intuitionism from psychology, logic and the study of languages and formal systems, which he all considered to be forms of applied mathematics.

As it turns out, various parts of classical mathematics cannot be reconstructed intuitionistically. Conversely, Brouwer introduced objects and principles of reasoning about them that are not acceptable in classical mathematics. For example, Intuitionism rejects Cantorian set theory and the universal validity of the Principle of the Excluded Middle, but introduces choice sequences. Brouwer used these to develop a constructive theory of the continuum that does not let it fall apart into atoms, as a set-theoretical analysis does. *See also* EXCLUDED MIDDLE, PRINCIPLE OF; FOUNDATIONS OF MATHEMATICS; HILBERT'S PROGRAMME; INTUITIONISM; RUSSELL'S PROGRAMME. [MVA]

Cardinality. The cardinality of a class is the number of its elements. A class has finite cardinality when the number of its elements is a natural number; it has transfinite cardinality, when it has infinitely many elements. The Principle of Extensionality states that two classes β and γ have the same cardinality if, and only if, there is a bijection between them, that is, if and only if their elements can be paired off together. *See also* CLASSES. [FB]

Categorical Proposition. *See* PROPOSITION.

Category. A category is a most general kind of predicate. For instance, an apple can be 'red' or 'green'; what is common to the two predicates 'red' and 'green' is their being a quality. Hence, quality is one of the most general features of the world, or at least of our conceptualization of the world. Aristotle found ten categories, but his method has been said to be more grammatical than logical. Discovering categories should indeed be a concern of the logical analysis of judgments: for example, *a*, *some* and *all* indicate that the three categories of quantity are unity, plurality and totality. *See also* PREDICATE; ARISTOTLE; PEIRCE, CHARLES SANDERS; ORGANON. [JMC]

Classes. A class is the collection of all things that have a certain property. Consider the property 'red': the collection of all red things is a class.

Some classes may be themselves members of classes, so that to this extent they are similar to sets. Classes which cannot be members of other classes, like the class of all sets, are called proper classes. *See also* PROPERTY; SET; SET THEORY. [FB]

Closed World Assumption. The assumption that what is not known to be true is false. In a knowledge base this assumption is correct when the database is complete. With incomplete information, the closed world assumption gives an approximate answer to a question. This answer can be wrong because not all information is taken into account. The closed world assumption is used in commercial SQL and XML databases and in logic programming. *See also* ASSUMPTION; LOGIC PROGRAMMING. [KV]

Coherence. In logic, coherence is synonymous with consistency. In semantics, coherence is exploited in order to provide a definition of truth. This definition is an alternative to the correspondence definition, which was first stated by

Aristotle and developed by Tarski. Within a coherence truth-theory, a proposition φ is true if and only if it is consistent with a given set Γ of propositions, that is, if no contradiction can be derived in case we add φ to Γ.

In Bayesian probability theory, an assignment of degrees of belief is said to be coherent if and only if it is not susceptible to Dutch book, that is, if and only if betting according to these degrees of belief does not open the bettor up to the possibility of loss whatever the outcome. *See also* CONSISTENCY, PROBABILITY, INTERPRETATION OF; PROPOSITION; SET; TRUTH; ARISTOTLE; TARSKI, ALFRED. [FB]

Completeness. *See* THEOREMS.

Complexity. There is no single, agreed upon definition of what it is to be complex, but rather a cluster of related notions covering both epistemological and ontological aspects of complexity. Of those most relevant to logic are definitions of algorithmic complexity arising from information theory, and applied to strings in some specified formal language. The best-established of this class of definitions is *Kolmogorov complexity* (KC). The KC of a string of binary digits is measured by the length of its shortest description. Thus the string '101010101010101010101010' can be (fully) described as '12 repetitions of "01"', whereas the most efficient way to describe a disordered string such as '011000101011101101100010' may be to write down the entire string. One implication of the KC measure is that random strings have the highest complexity. They are also *incompressible* in the sense that there is no way of providing a specification of a random string that is shorter than the string itself. To make the KC measure precise, it must be relativized to a particular (formal) language of description. A quite separate notion of complexity in logic, sometimes known as *quantifier complexity*, measures the complexity of propositions in predicate logic based on the number of alternating blocks of quantifiers occurring in the proposition. *See also* LOGIC, PREDICATE; PROPOSITION; QUANTIFIER. [ABa]

Computability. A function is computable when it is calculable in a definite (i.e., algorithmic) way in a finite number of steps. A set is computable when its characteristic function (the function f such that $f(x)=1$ when x belongs to the set) is computable. Several precise definitions have been proposed in order to explicate this somewhat vague notion, as a result of the works of Church, Gödel, Kleene and Turing. Computable functions have been defined in terms of recursive functions, Turing machines, and Lambda calculus. All these definitions turned out to be exactly coextensive. Recognizing these equivalences, the Church-Turing thesis states that a function is computable when it is calculable by a Turing machine (or, equivalently, when it is a recursive function). The Church-Turing thesis offers a rigorous explanation of computable functions; the thesis, which is generally accepted, can be neither proved nor refuted because it is an explication of an informal notion. A consequence of the Church-Turing thesis is that computable functions are those functions calculable by computers, which are physical realizations of a universal Turing machine.

There is a strong connection between computability and decidability: A theory is decidable when the set of its valid formulae is computable. In 1936 Turing, answering in the negative the decision problem for predicate logic posed by Hilbert, constructed a non-computable set of natural numbers by means of a diagonal argument similar to those previously employed by Cantor and Gödel. In this way Turing proved the existence of clearly defined non-computable functions. See also DECIDABILITY; LOGIC, PREDICATE; RECURSION; SET; TURING MACHINE; CANTOR, GEORG; CHURCH, ALONZO; GÖDEL, KURT; HILBERT, DAVID; TURING, ALAN. [MMu]

Conclusion. The conclusion of an argument is the proposition which is (supposed to be) supported by the argument's premisses. Every argument has only one conclusion, but the conclusion of one argument can be a premiss in another. In a valid deductive argument, the truth of the conclusion is forced by the truth of the premisses. See also ARGUMENT; DEDUCTION; INDUCTION; PREMISS; VALIDITY. [APM]

Condition, Necessary and Sufficient. Necessary and sufficient conditions can clarify the relationships between events (or properties, or facts). Let us call an event we are interested in, E. (Construe 'event' very broadly: buying groceries, winning the lottery, living abroad etc.) Suppose that whenever something else happens, then E happens. This 'something else' is then a sufficient condition for E. Call this condition S. Say E is 'being a dog'. Then one S might be 'being a beagle'. If x is a beagle, then x is a dog. We symbolize this relationship as: $S \rightarrow E$.

Now suppose that whenever E happens, something else always occurs. This 'something else' is then a necessary condition for E. Call this N. Say E is 'being fluent in German'. One N might be 'having learned German'. One cannot be fluent in German without having learned it. If *x* is fluent in German, then *x* learned it. We might symbolize this relationship as: $E{\to}N$.

If you have a lottery ticket and you have picked the winning numbers, then you will win the lottery. If we take *E* to be 'your winning', then we see that 'having a ticket' (*H*) and 'picking the winning numbers' (*P*) together form a sufficient condition for *E*. The two conditions are jointly sufficient (($H{\wedge}P){\to}E$). Each on its own, however, is not sufficient.

While driving my car, I know it has fuel in it and that its engine works. If *E* is 'I'm driving my car' then 'having fuel in it and its engine working' ($F{\wedge}W$) is a necessary condition for *E* ('$E{\to}(F{\wedge}W)$'). Here, however, each conjunct can be taken individually as a necessary condition of *E* ('$E{\to}F$' and '$E{\to}W$').

Conditions needn't be classified only in one way. Consider 'winning the lottery', above. Having a ticket and picking the right numbers ($H{\wedge}P$) is necessary, as well as sufficient, for winning the lottery. *See also* ANTECEDENT; CONDITIONAL; CONSEQUENT; CONJUNCTION. [CF]

Conditional. *See* IMPLICATION.

Conjecture. A mathematical statement which is considered likely to be true, but has resisted all attempts to prove or disprove it formally. When a conjecture has been proven, it is promoted to the status of a theorem. When a counterexample has been found, the conjecture is merely a false conjecture. *See also* COUNTEREXAMPLE; THEOREM. [KV]

Conjunction. A conjunction is a compound statement of the form '*P* and *Q*', written $P{\wedge}Q$. We usually form the conjunction of two statements by inserting the word 'and' between them. For example, It is sunny (*P*) and ($\wedge$) the children are outdoors (*Q*). *P* and *Q* are called conjuncts. Conjunction is truth-functional: $P{\wedge}Q$ takes the value true if and only if both conjuncts are true. Conjunction introduction, a rule of inference of the form *P*, *Q*, $\therefore$ $P{\wedge}Q$, is used for deriving a conjunction. The various logical symbols employed to represent conjunction as a connective include the following; $\wedge$, κ, $\bullet$ and &. *See also* CONNECTIVES; TRUTH-TABLE. [JB]

Connectives. A basic logical unit is the complete sentence without logical complexity, such as 'Old films are good'. Connectives are used to combine these basic logical units to produce logically complex statements. These complex statements are then capable of combination by connectives as well.

We can classify connectives by the number of 'holes' they have to be filled. 'Not' ('It is not the case that___') has one hole; it is called a 1-place connective. 'And' is a 2-place connective. The result of filling in the blanks with complete sentences (simple or complex) is always a (more complex) complete sentence. Note that there are no restrictions on which sentences one may use to fill in the blank(s).

The standard five connectives are 'not', 'and', 'or', 'if . . . then . . . ' and 'if and only if'. Thus we can build (1) 'if old films aren't good then I'll eat my hat', which we may symbolize as (2) '$\neg A_1 \rightarrow A_2$'. Two connectives appear in (1) and (2): 'if . . . then . . . ' and 'not'.

There are many other connectives. Consider the 2-place connective 'Although ___ it is false that ___'. This is a connective, but it's not one that's very common. 'Neither ___ nor ___' is another that is, however. *See also* BICONDITIONAL; CONDITIONAL; CONJUNCTION; DISJUNCTION; NEGATION. [CF]

Consequent. One of the two logical parts of a conditional statement, often preceded by a 'then'. Consider: 'If you laugh, then I'll scream'. The consequent here is 'I'll scream' because the consequence of you laughing is that I will scream (if the conditional is true). Whatever plays this logical role is the consequent. *See also* ANTECEDENT; CONDITIONAL; IMPLICATION, MATERIAL. [CF]

Consistency. A set Γ of sentences is said to be syntactically consistent if, and only if, there is no sentence φ such that both φ and $\neg\varphi$ are derivable from Γ. A set Γ of sentences is said to be semantically consistent if, and only if, there is no sentence φ such that both φ and $\neg\varphi$ are logical consequences of Γ. We may also say that a set Γ of sentences is semantically consistent if, and only if, it has a model, which is if and only if there is an interpretation of Γ that makes every element of Γ true.

In 1931, Kurt Gödel showed that the system Russell and Whitehead proposed in *Principia Mathematica* for the derivation of mathematics on a purely logical basis cannot prove its own consistency. As a matter of fact, every first-order logical system augmented by Peano axioms for arithmetic cannot prove its own consistency. This result is known as Gödel's second incompleteness theorem. *See also* INTERPRETATION; LOGICAL CONSEQUENCE; MODEL; SENTENCES; SET; GÖDEL, KURT; RUSSELL, BERTRAND; PRINCIPIA MATHEMATICA. [FB]

Constructive Dilemma. *See* INFERENCE, RULES OF.

Contingent. A formula φ is contingent if and only if it is neither necessary (i.e., necessarily true), nor impossible (i.e., necessarily false). This condition can be written: $\Diamond\varphi \leftrightarrow (\neg\Box\varphi \wedge \neg\Box\neg\varphi)$, where the diamond signifies 'is contingent' and the box signifies 'necessarily'. *See also* NECESSITY. [FS]

Contradiction. A sentence φ is a contradiction if and only if it is logically impossible that it is true or, equivalently, it is logically necessary that it is false. In other words, no interpretation of φ can be given such that it is a model of φ. A sentence of the form $\psi \wedge \neg\psi$ is a contradiction, for instance 'My shirt is red and my shirt is not red.' The symbol for the contradiction is $\bot$.

The Principle of Non-Contradiction states that the proposition expressed by the sentence φ cannot be true and false at the same time. *See also* CONSISTENCY; INTERPRETATION; MODEL; SENTENCE. [FB]

Contraposition. *See* SQUARE OF OPPOSITION.

Corollary. A statement which can be inferred immediately from a previously proven theorem with little or no additional derivation. A corollary can be accompanied by a proof if the derivation needs some insight; if the author considers the derivation self-evident, the proof is left to the reader. *See also* PROOF; THEOREM. [KV]

Countable. A set A is countable if each object in A can be assigned a unique natural number. Such a set can be either finite or infinite. For example, the set of even numbers is both infinite and countable. Cantor showed that the set of real numbers is not countable. *See also* SET THEORY; CANTOR, GEORG. [AH]

Counterexample. In a (deductive) argument that is valid, the premise(s) (taken together) imply the conclusion. An invalid argument admits of a counterexample. A counterexample is an interpretation of the terms in the argument that suffices to show that the inference from the premise(s) (taken together) to the conclusion fails. Practically, this amounts to demonstrating that the premisses of the argument can each be true while the conclusion is false.

Consider the following argument, (1): 'If CF wrote this argument, then electricity was used; electricity was used; therefore, CF wrote this argument'. (1) is invalid, and we can show this with a counterexample. Suppose that electricity was used, but that someone else wrote (1). This would show that I can make the argument's premisses true while its conclusion is false. That this situation is logically possible shows that the argument is invalid. My supposed situation constitutes a counterexample.

Now consider (2): 'If CF wrote this argument, then electricity was used; CF wrote this argument; therefore, electricity was used'. (2) differs from (1) with respect to logical form. If we assume the premisses to be true, then we cannot make the conclusion false. There is no counterexample; (2) is valid. *See also* ARGUMENT; INFERENCE; IMPLICATION; INTERPRETATION; INVALIDITY; VALIDITY. [CF]

Counterfactual. *See* IMPLICATION, COUNTERFACTUAL.

De Morgan, Laws of. This law, first stated by Ockham but so-called after Augustus de Morgan, allows one to replace one expression by another. It entails two logical rules which form part of standard propositional logic. The first rule states that ¬(p∧q) is logically equivalent to ¬p ∨ ¬q. The second states that ¬(p ∨ q) is equivalent to ¬p ∧ ¬q. In plain English, these rules state that (1) the negation of a conjunction implies, and is implied by, the disjunction of the negated conjuncts and (2) the negation of a disjunction implies, and is implied by, the conjunction of the negated disjuncts. *See also* DE MORGAN, AUGUSTUS. [JB]

De Re / De Dicto. The *de re / de dicto* distinction appears most frequently in discussions of modal logic and propositional attitude ascriptions, where statements exhibit an ambiguity between a *de re* reading and *de dicto* reading. Interpreted *de re*, modal claims ascribe modal properties to things (*res*) while interpreted *de dicto*, such claims hold that it is sentences (*dicta*) that are necessarily or possibly true. Consider, for instance, 'The number of continents is necessarily odd.' Taken *de re*, this claim ascribes the property *necessary oddness* to the number 7 (the number which is in fact the number of the continents). Taken *de dicto*, this claim asserts that the sentence 'There is an odd number of continents' is necessarily true. The *de re* reading is plausible (how could 7 not be odd?), but, given that it is possible there were only 6 continents, the *de dicto* reading is false.

Propositional attitude ascriptions also exhibit a *de re / de dicto* ambiguity. Read *de re*, the sentence 'Ben believes someone is a spy' claims that Ben suspects a particular person (say, his friend Sophie) of being a spy, while interpreted *de dicto*, it claims merely that Ben believes there are spies. *See also* LOGIC, MODAL; NECESSITY; SCOPE. [APM]

Decidability. A formal system *T* – that is, a system that consists of a formalized language, a set of axioms and a set of inference rules – is decidable when the set of its valid formulae (those sentences that are true in all possible interpretations) is computable; that is, *T* is decidable when there exists an algorithm that decides, for every formula of *T*, whether the formula is valid. Computability theory states that *T* is decidable when the set of its valid formulae is recursive (computable by a Turing machine).

Well-known decidable logical theories are propositional logic, in which truth-tables provide an algorithm to decide the validity of every formula, and first-order monadic predicate logic, which deals with predicates with only one argument. Other decidable theories are the theory of real closed fields, elementary Euclidean geometry, and the fragment of Peano arithmetic without multiplication.

Hilbert, who believed that mathematics is decidable, considered the problem of finding a decision algorithm for first-order predicate logic (the so-called decision problem) as the main problem of mathematical logic. The decision problem was solved by Church and Turing independently in 1936. They proved that first-order predicate logic is not decidable. In this case, there exists an algorithm such that, for every formula A, if A is valid then the algorithm will find a proof of A; however, if A is not valid, there is no algorithm that will always find a counterexample to A. In other words, there exists a Turing machine such that, if one gives a valid formula A as input, the Turing machine will halt outputting a proof of A; but there are infinitely many non-valid formulae B such that, if one gives B as input, the Turing machine will never halt. This result can be stated in another equivalent way: The set of valid formulae is recursively enumerable while the set of satisfiable formulae is not recursively enumerable. *See also* AXIOM; COMPLETENESS; COMPUTABILITY; FORMAL SYSTEM; LOGIC, PREDICATE; LOGIC, PROPOSITIONAL; RECURSION; TRUTH-TABLE; TURING MACHINE; VALIDITY; CHURCH, ALONZO; HILBERT, DAVID; TURING, ALAN. [MMu]

Deduction. Deduction can be characterized as necessary inference. It is widely, though not universally, accepted that deduction is a transition from (at least one) premise(s) to a conclusion, such that it is impossible for the former to be (jointly) true and the conclusion false. Note that false premisses can lead in a deductively valid way to a true conclusion, for example, Napoleon was Indian; All Indians are conquerors ∴ Napoleon was a conqueror – constituting an unsound argument. Validity of deductive arguments is widely taken to depend exclusively on logical relations between sentences, rather than substantive relations between the contents they express. Importantly, the content of the conclusion of a deductively valid argument is uninformative relative to the content of the premise-set. In a deductive argument, one cannot (i) *increase* the (informational) content of the conclusion above that of the premise-set; nor (ii) *decrease* said content by adding more restrictive premisses: If A implies B, then $A \wedge C$ still implies B (monotony); nor (iii) *order* premisses according to their contents' importance: Should premisses believed to be true deductively imply a false conclusion, then – logically – each premise is equally revisable; nor (iv) *validate* premises by means of a true conclusion which is deductively implied. *See also* ARGUMENT; CONCLUSION; FALLACY; INDUCTION; INFERENCE, RULES OF; LOGIC, NONMONOTONIC; PREMISS; SOUNDNESS; SYLLOGISM; TAUTOLOGY; VALIDITY. [FZ]

Definite Description. A definite description is an expression that can be used to pick out exactly one thing. 'The current president of France' is a definite description that picks out one unique individual. Definite descriptions often employ the definite article 'the'.

Bertrand Russell gave an analysis of the truth of definite descriptions: (1) something must exist that has the described characteristics, and (2) it must be the only thing having those characteristics. 'The current president of France is not bald' is true when: (1) there is a current president of France who's not bald, and (2) no one else is the current president of France. *See also* IDENTITY; QUANTIFIER. [CF]

Dilemma. Situation in which one of two propositions must be true, each of which yields a (typically unattractive) consequence. Generalizes to: tri-, tetra-, polylemma. Formally: $A \lor B, A \rightarrow C, B \rightarrow C \therefore C$. The conditional premisses are called the horns of the dilemma. 'Escaping between the horns' amounts to denying the disjunction by showing a third alternative that does not yield the undesired consequence. 'Taking it by the horns' amounts to denying at least one of the conditionals. In contrast to a false dilemma (fallacy), neither strategy will succeed in the case of a sound dilemma. *See also* DISJUNCTION; FALLACY; INFERENCE, RULES OF; PROPOSITION. [FZ]

Disjunction. Disjunction is a compound statement of the form of 'P or Q', written $P \lor Q$. Each component of such a statement is a disjunct. Disjunction is used both in the exclusive and inclusive sense. When we say 'P or Q', we often mean the same as 'exactly one of P and Q'. This truth-function is commonly called exclusive disjunction. On the other hand, 'P or Q' can mean 'either or both of both P and Q'; this is inclusive disjunction . Inclusive disjunction takes the value False if both disjuncts are false, and otherwise takes the value True. This distinction can be captured by a truth-table. The symbol '$\lor$', now called the wedge or 'vel', is often employed to represent this truth-function. *See also* INFERENCE, RULES OF; TRUTH-TABLE. [JB]

Disjunctive Normal Form. A standardized representation of a logical formula, expressed as a disjunction of conjunctions. Each conjunction in the disjunctive normal form contains only atomic propositions or their negations. As a consequence, the only permitted propositional operators in the normal form are *and*, *or* and *not*. Each logical formula has a disjunctive normal form. An example of a logical formula in disjunctive normal form is $(\neg A \wedge B) \vee (A \wedge C)$. *See also* CONJUNCTION; DISJUNCTION; NORMAL FORM; PROPOSITION. [KV]

Disjunctive Syllogism. *See* INFERENCE, RULES OF.

Domain. The domain of a function is the set of the entities the function takes as arguments. The domain of discourse is the class of entities a theory speaks of. In logical theories, the domain is the class of entities the variables of the theory take as values. *See also* CLASSES; INTERPRETATION; SET; VARIABLE. [FB]

Double Negation. *See* CONNECTIVES.

Entailment. See DEDUCTION, LOGICAL CONSEQUENCE.

Euler Diagrams. Euler diagrams represent categorical propositions as pairs of circles, overlapping partially, wholly or not at all. Leonhard Euler (1707–1783) popularized them in *Lettres à une princesse d'Allemagne* (vol. 1, 1768. St. Petersburg: L'Académie Impériale des Sciences), overlooking anticipations by Leibniz and others. Three circle Euler diagrams evaluate syllogisms, but clumsily compared with their offspring, Venn diagrams.

Figure 1 All A are B.

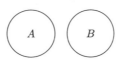

Figure 2 No A are B.

Figure 3 Some A are B.

Figure 4 Some A are not B.

See also PROPOSITION; VENN DIAGRAMS. [AA]

Excluded Middle, Principle of. The principle of excluded middle is one of the defining properties of classical systems of logic, and is part of the rules of thought in Aristotle's *Metaphysics*. The other principles are the principles of identity and that of non-contradiction. The principle states that the disjunction of any statement with its negation is always true: for any proposition *P*, either

P or *not-P*, written (P∨¬P). For example, 'either there is a tree over 300 feet tall or it is not the case that there is a tree over 300 feet tall' must be true.

This principle should not be confused with the principle of bivalence, a meta-logical principle which states that there are two and only two truth-values, true and false, and that, for any proposition *P*, *P* can only have one of these truth-values. *See also* BIVALENCE. [JB]

Existential Generalization. *See* QUANTIFICATION RULES.

Existential Instantiation. *See* QUANTIFICATION RULES.

Existential Quantifier. A logical operator in predicate logic expressing that a property or relation holds for at least one element of the domain. The existential quantifier is denoted by the symbol ∃, a rotated letter 'E'. For example, the formula ∃x (x > 0) asserts the existence of some value x greater than 0. *See also* DOMAIN; EXISTENTIAL GENERALIZATION; EXISTENTIAL INSTANTIATION; LOGICAL OPERATOR; LOGIC, PREDICATE. [KV]

Extension. An extension is the set of all things that have a given property: the extension of the property *P* is the set of all individuals that have *P*. It also indicates the semantic value of a given expression under a given interpretation. *See also* INTERPRETATION; PROPERTY; SEMANTICS; SET. [FB]

Fallacy. A fallacy is an argument which, though plausible, is defective. 'Argument' is here used in the broad sense of a contribution to a dialogue, in which reasons are advanced. There are rules for the proper conduct of an argument. To commit a fallacy is to perpetrate (accidentally or deliberately) a subtle violation of one or other of those rules.

There are many types of argumentative misconduct and, correspondingly, many types of fallacy. For example, an opponent should not be bullied into accepting anything. To break this rule by insinuating some kind of a threat into one's argument is to commit the fallacy *Argumentum ad Baculum* – an appeal to force. Appeal to an authority (especially when that authority is not an authority on the matter under discussion) is the fallacy *Argumentum ad Verecundiam*. Appealing to popular opinion (*Argumentum ad Populum*) is fallacious, not so much because public opinion is frequently mistaken, as because citing the widely held opinion in favour of a view does not amount to supplying a solid *argument* showing that view to be true.

An obvious rule of argumentative conduct is that we should express ourselves in such a way that we are not likely to be misunderstood. We commit the fallacy of *Equivocation* when one or more of the words used in the argument is ambiguous, leaving ourselves open to being interpreted in more than one way. Sometimes a sentence can be susceptible of two or more interpretations not because any of the words in it are ambiguous but because it may be parsed in two or more ways. Example: 'Fighting kangaroos can be fun'. Argumentative error that arises from a confusing of such interpretations is known as the fallacy of *Amphiboly*.

Another rule for good argument is that the premisses should be relevant to establishing the conclusion. Some fallacies arise when premisses that might seem to be relevant or adequate to establishing the conclusion are in fact irrelevant or inadequate:

Post Hoc Ergo Propter Hoc (After this, therefore on account of this). It is a fallacy to think that if one event occurs after another, the earlier accounts for, or causes, the later. It may be true that, after schools started employing educational psychologists, the rate of teenage drug abuse and crime rose. But it does not follow that employing educational psychologists was responsible for this rise.

Petitio Principii (also known as Begging the Question or Circular Argumentation). This fallacy occurs when one of the reasons given in the course of an argument is identical to, or just a linguistic variant on, the very conclusion one is trying to draw. The simplest example of this is when premise and conclusion are equivalent, for example 'It is best to have government by the people because democracy is the best form of government'. But much more complicated cases are usual. (Note that there is a widespread but mistaken tendency to think that 'to beg the question' means 'to raise the question'. To beg the question is to argue for a particular answer in a way that presupposes the truth of that answer.)

Hasty Generalization. The mistake of drawing a general conclusion from a small number of possibly atypical instances. That John Stuart Mill and Bertrand Russell profited greatly from a private education does not imply that all children would benefit from being educated at home.

Straw Man. In this fallacy your argument is relevant to establishing a conclusion subtly different from the conclusion you are purporting to establish. Suppose the bus company wants to raise its fares by 20%. That will hit you badly in the pocket, and you write a long letter to the company arguing that a 20% increase in the cost of living would be economically ruinous. But neither the bus company nor anyone else is proposing a 20% increase in the general cost of living. So your letter is aiming at the wrong target, one of your own contrivance, a straw man.

Argumentum ad Ignorantiam. The fallacy of arguing from the fact that we don't know whether something is true to the conclusion that it is false. It may be true, for example, that none of the research that has been done on the subject of pornography has established that it does harm to women. So we don't know whether pornography does harm to women. But it would be fallacious to conclude that pornography does not harm women.

Denying the Antecedent. Consider 'If Beavis continues to smoke, he will die within three years. Beavis does not continue to smoke. Therefore he will not die within three years.' This might seem to be a valid argument, but it is not – the premisses could be true while the conclusion is false. This is a formal fallacy – any argument of the same form (If A then B. Not-A. Therefore Not-B) is fallacious. Another formal fallacy is *Affirming the Consequent* (If A then B. B. Therefore A.)

Logicians study fallacies (of which the above is but a small sample) because it is useful to identify and categorize the ways in which we ought *not* to reason, and the classification of fallacies is usually in terms of the type of logical error they exhibit. However, psychological experiments have shown that, when reasoning about factual matters, humans are subject to diverse biases and misconceptions. We could, perhaps more fruitfully, classify fallacies according to their psychological roots. It should be possible to find deep evolutionary explanations for the various sorts of argumentative errors we are prone to commit. Revealing the ways we go wrong is very revealing of the kind of animal we are.

In his excellent compendium of fallacies *How to Win Every Argument* (2006: Continuum), Madsen Pirie recommends arming oneself with the impressive Latin names of fallacies before doing argumentative battle: 'When an opponent is accused of perpetrating something with a Latin name it sounds as if he is suffering from a rare tropical disease. It has the added effect of making the accuser seem both erudite and authoritative'. *See also* ANTECEDENT; ARGUMENT; ARGUMENTATION, THEORY OF; CONCLUSION; CONSEQUENT; PREMISS; TRUTH; VALIDITY; MILL, JOHN STUART; RUSSELL, BERTRAND. [LG]

Forcing. In 1938, Kurt Gödel showed that it was impossible to disprove the Continuum Hypothesis. Cantor's Continuum Hypothesis, introduced in 1877, proposes that there is no set whose size is between that of the integers and that of the real numbers. In 1963 Paul Cohen extended this result by proving that both the Continuum Hypothesis and the Axiom of Choice are undecidable in Zermelo-Fraenkel set theory. Cohen's proofs relied on a technique he invented, called 'forcing', where statements that are declared true initially must continue to remain true as the set-theoretic model is built. Cohen's method of forcing is a powerful problem-solving tool in many areas of mathematics including set theory. *See also* AXIOM; PROOF. [DH]

Formal System. A formal system consists of a formal language together with a proof procedure.

A formal language has two parts: a collection of symbols, which we call its alphabet; and a set of grammatical rules, which specify how we may combine these symbols to produce well-formed formulae (or wffs) of the language. For example:

Alphabet:

    L: {#, &}.

Grammatical rules:

    GR1:   # is a wff.

    GR2:   If φ is a wff, then φ& is a wff (where φ is a string of symbols from L).

Given a formal language, sometimes we wish to pick out a collection of its wffs. Suppose T is such a collection. Sometimes the best or only way of picking out T is by specifying two things: a set of wffs (called axioms) that belong to T, but (usually) do not exhaust it; and a set of rules (called rules of inference) by which all the wffs in T may be derived from the axioms. Together, a set of axioms and a set of rules of inference constitute a proof procedure. For example:

Axioms:

    A1:   #&&

Rules of inference:

    RI1:   From φ&, derive φ (where φ is a wff).

Together L, GR1–2, A1 and RI1 constitute a formal system. *See also* AXIOM; INFERENCE; PROOF. [RP]

Foundations of Mathematics. What is the nature and meaning of mathematics, and how do these relate to its practice? The joint technical and philosophical investigation of these questions is now known as foundations of mathematics. Foundations, then, has the formal job of providing and describing the objects of mathematics, such as sets, numbers and functions, and the philosophical job of explaining mathematics – proof, truth and the relations between the two.

Foundations is itself a branch of mathematics, because it formally studies subjects like proof and truth by proving theorems about them. And foundations is a branch of philosophy, because proof and truth are core concepts for rational inquiry and argument.

Modern foundational studies can be traced to Frege and Russell, who, in advancing their thesis of logicism, pioneered some very general tools and provided a strong early map of the conceptual landscape for others to follow.

Following that revolution in logic at the turn of the twentieth century, foundational studies have been associated with set theory, where numbers, functions and their properties are built up step by step from a few basic axioms about collections, in the style of Euclid. For a foundation to provide the objects of mathematics usually means to prove that there are such objects, in the sense of proving that 'there is a natural number successor for every natural number'.

Foundational studies matured during a crisis, triggered by the appearance of various paradoxes threatening the consistency of logic itself. The most well known of these was Russell's paradox, announced in 1902. Another crisis in the foundations is said to have occurred in ancient Greece, upon the discovery of irrational numbers, then called incommensurable magnitudes; at that time no provisions were yet in place for quantities not representable by whole-number ratios. A crisis, then, is characterized by basic elements being not clearly defined or adequately understood. A secure foundation, by contrast, clearly illuminates the meanings and uses of core mathematical concepts.

Following Hilbert, a foundation of mathematics is often expected to be a formal system. An ideal such system would produce a theory to meet the criteria of Hilbert's programme – of being consistent (for no sentence A is $A \wedge \neg A$ provable), complete (for any sentence A, either A is provable or $\neg A$ is provable), and categorical (the theory has only one model, up to isomorphism). If all this could be done, the theory would in effect be a universal mathematical truth machine, capable of mechanically producing all and only the theorems of mathematics. In 1899 Hilbert succeeded in carrying out his programme with geometry, but following Gödel's theorem in 1931, it has been known that not all the criteria are co-tenable for branches of mathematics at or above the level of arithmetic.

The most ambitious attempts to provide a foundation were Russell and Whitehead's *Principia Mathematica* published in three hefty volumes from 1910 to 1913, and Bourbaki's *Eléments de mathématique*. *See also* AXIOM; FORMAL SYSTEM; HILBERT'S PROGRAMME; LOGICISM; SET THEORY; FREGE, GOTTLOB; RUSSELL, BERTAND; PRINCIPIA MATHEMATICA. [ZW]

Hilbert's programme. Hilbert's programme was one of the three major responses to the foundational crisis in mathematics of the early twentieth century. In contrast to Russell's logicism and Brouwer's intuitionism, Hilbert's programme, also called formalism, viewed mathematics purely as a meaningless formal system and so the task was to find such a system within which all, and only, true mathematical statements could be derived. In addition, a proof of the consistency of this axiomatization of mathematics is required, using what Hilbert referred to as 'finitary methods'. Hilbert was unwilling to accept Cantor's view whereby infinite sets were treated as completed objects or entities in their own right and so he used the term 'finitary' to refer to methods that did not depend on the existence of these infinite totalities.

This was the downfall of Hilbert's programme since, following Gödel's proofs, it was generally accepted that no finitary consistency proof of arithmetic can be given.

However, some researchers, for example Solomon Feferman, have continued to work on a modified formalism, known as Relativized Hilbert programmes, which have been influential in proof theory.

For a philosophical discussion of these issues *See* Detlefsen, Michael, 1990, 'On an alleged refutation of Hilbert's programme using Gödel's first incompleteness theorem', *Journal of Philosophical Logic*, 19: 343–77. *See also* AXIOM; INTUITIONISM; FORMAL SYSTEM; LOGICISM. [DH]

Hypothesis. Arguments start from hypotheses, that is, from propositions, be they true or false, that are in that context assumed for the sake of argument without further proof. Analogously, some deductive systems allow the introduction of arbitrary well-formed formulae as hypotheses. Reasoning from hypotheses can establish conditional (or hypothetical) conclusions of the form: *If* the hypotheses are true, *then* such and such. In an indirect proof, one hypothesis will be refuted through the derivation of an absurd, clearly false or even impossible conclusion. *See also* ARGUMENT; CONCLUSION; IMPLICATION; PROOF; PROPOSITION. [LJ]

Hypothetical Syllogism. *See* INFERENCE, RULES OF.

Identity. Identity is the unique relation in which each thing stands to itself. When the generic relation symbol of predicate logic 'R' is used to express the two-place identity relation, the notation '$R(x,y)$' is usually substituted with '$x=y$', and the latter expression means that the symbols 'x' and 'y' refer to the same thing. Identity is typically regarded as a primitive. However, Leibniz contended that it is derivative on the qualities of things, so that each thing differs from every other with respect to at least one property, and this determines its unique identity. This view was developed in the twentieth century by Hilbert and Bernays and by Quine. While identity as defined above is not relative to anything, and is consequently called 'absolute identity', it is sometimes held that identity must be relative to some concept. That is, in asserting that x and y are the same, an answer to the question 'The same what?' must also be specified. According to some (e.g. Geach) there is only relative identity. *See also* LOGIC; LOGIC, PREDICATE; PROPERTY; LEIBNIZ, GOTTFRIED WILHELM; QUINE, WILLARD VAN ORMAN. [MMo]

Identity of the Indiscernibles. The Identity of the Indiscernibles is the principle, first explicitly formulated by Leibniz, according to which there cannot be two things identical in every respect. Differently put, the principle states that if two entities have all the same properties, they are in fact the same entity. Unlike the closely related principle of the Indiscernibility of the Identicals, this principle is not an axiom of logic and is in fact quite controversial. Leibniz took for granted that different things exist at different places and contended that there must be some additional intrinsic difference (e.g. two leaves found in different parts of a garden must also differ with respect to at least one other property: for instance, a tiny particular regarding their shapes). Nowadays, a weaker form of the principle, making a difference in location sufficient for non-identity, is commonly assumed. In reaction to certain thought-experimental and actual counterexamples, moreover, some Quinean insights have been revived very recently with a view to formulating an even weaker version of the principle, based on relations rather than monadic properties. *See also* AXIOM; INDISCERNIBILITY OF THE IDENTICALS; PROPERTY; LEIBNIZ, GOTTFRIED WILHELM. [MMo]

Implication. A binary relation that holds between sentences (or propositions) and corresponds to the English expression 'if . . . then . . . '. (Implication can also be thought of as a connective or logical function.) To say that φ implies ψ is to make the conditional claim that if φ is (or were) true, then ψ is (or would be) true. In formal systems, implication is typically symbolized using '→' or '⊃'. A necessary (but not sufficient) condition for such a connective's expressing implication is that it satisfy modus ponens; that is, that from φ → ψ and φ one may infer ψ. *See also* ANTECEDENT; BINARY; CONNECTIVES; CONSEQUENT; IMPLICATION, INDICATIVE; IMPLICATION, MATERIAL; IMPLICATION, SUBJUNCTIVE; FORMAL SYSTEM; LOGICAL FUNCTION; MODUS PONENS; PROPOSITION. [CMG]

Implication, Causal. A type of implication. To say that φ causally implies ψ is to say that φ is causally sufficient for ψ – that is, if φ is (or were) true, then ψ is (or would be) true because φ is true. For example, to say that 'Alice stubs her toe' causally implies 'Alice feels pain' is to say that if Alice stubs her toe then this will cause her to feel pain. An important feature of causal implication is that it is not truth-functional. *See also* IMPLICATION; IMPLICATION, SUBJUNCTIVE; TRUTH-FUNCTIONAL. [CMG]

Implication, Counterfactual. A type of subjunctive implication in which the antecedent is presupposed to be false. To say that φ counterfactually implies ψ is to say that if, contrary to fact, φ were true, then ψ would be true. An example of a counterfactual statement is 'If Hitler had been killed in the early 1930s, World War II would not have occurred.' *See also* ANTECEDENT; IMPLICATION; IMPLICATION, SUBJUNCTIVE. [CMG]

Implication, Indicative. A type of implication corresponding to the English expression 'if . . . then . . . ' when used in what linguists call the *indicative* mood. To say that φ indicatively implies ψ is to say that if φ is, in fact, true, then ψ is, in fact, true. Arguably, indicative conditionals are truth-functional, and thus can be formalized using material implication. To see the difference between indicative and subjunctive implication, contrast the following conditional statements: (i) 'If Shakespeare did not write *Hamlet*, then someone else did' (indicative, probably true); (ii) 'If Shakespeare had not written *Hamlet*, then someone else would have' (subjunctive, probably false). *See also* IMPLICATION; IMPLICATION, MATERIAL; IMPLICATION, SUBJUNCTIVE; TRUTH-FUNCTIONAL. [CMG]

Implication, Material. A binary logical operator, written as $X \to Y$, which is commonly read as 'if X, then Y' in natural language. Its truth-value is *false* when X is *true* and Y is *false*, and *true* otherwise. It is logically equivalent to $\neg X \vee Y$. X is called the antecedent of the implication and Y the consequent.

The 'if X, then Y' reading is not completely correct: a more exact translation in natural language would be 'it is false that X is true when Y is false'. Any material implication with a false antecedent is true, for example 'If the moon is made of green cheese, then life exists on other planets.' Moreover, any material implication with a true consequent is true, for example, 'If life exists on other planets, then life exists on earth.' Both these sentences are true under material implication, which violates our intuitions of the meaning of 'if . . . then . . . ' However, in other expressions in natural language people do recognize that anything follows from a false antecedent, for example when we say 'If Jones wins the election this time, then I'm the Pope.' Instead of asserting the falsehood of Jones winning the election, we say that if the antecedent holds, anything follows, even an absurdity. *See also* ANTECEDENT; BINARY; CONSEQUENT; LOGICAL OPERATOR. [KV]

Implication, Strict. A type of implication that asserts a necessary connection between the antecedent and consequent. To say that φ strictly implies ψ is to say that, as a matter of necessity, if φ is true, then ψ is true. In (alethic) modal logic the claim that φ strictly implies ψ can be expressed as $(\varphi \rightarrow \psi)$. Interpreting certain if-then statements in terms of strict implication, rather than the weaker material implication, allows one to avoid certain (alleged) paradoxes. For example, a contingently false statement like 'Snow is black' materially implies, but does not strictly imply, '$0 = 1$'. *See also* ANTECEDENT; CONSEQUENT; CONTINGENT; IMPLICATION; IMPLICATION, MATERIAL; LOGIC, MODAL; NECESSITY; PARADOX. [CMG]

Implication, Subjunctive. A non-truth-functional variety of implication corresponding to the English expression 'If . . . then . . . ' when used in (what linguists call) the subjunctive mood. To say that φ subjunctively implies ψ is to say that if φ were true, then ψ would be true. (Contrast this with indicative implication.) An example of a subjunctive conditional is 'If Alice were to win the lottery, she would be ecstatic'. Subjunctive implication is sometimes equated with counterfactual implication, but there is an important difference: the antecedent of a subjunctive conditional need not be presupposed to be false. (e.g. Alice may indeed win the lottery.) *See also* ANTECEDENT; IMPLICATION; IMPLICATION, CAUSAL; IMPLICATION, COUNTERFACTUAL; IMPLICATION, INDICATIVE; TRUTH-FUNCTIONAL. [CMG]

Independence. A sentence *A* is independent of a set of sentences Γ if and only if each of *A* and *not-A* is consistent with Γ. Independence results have been important in the history of logic and mathematics. Euclid's fifth postulate is independent of absolute geometry (Beltrami, E. 1868. 'Saggio di interpretazione della geometria non-euclidea'. *Giornale di Mathematiche*, 285–315). For every consistent and recursively enumerable and sufficiently rich theory, there is a statement in its language which is independent of it (Gödel, K. 1931. 'Über formal unentscheidbare Sätze der Principia Mathematica und verwandter Systeme, I'. *Monatshefte für Mathematik und Physik*, 38: 173–98). The Axiom of Choice and the Continuum Hypothesis are independent of Zermelo-Frankel set theory (Gödel, K. 1940. *The Consistency of the Axiom of Choice and of the Generalized Continuum Hypothesis with the Axioms of Set Theory*. Princeton University Press; Cohen, P.J. 1963. 'The independence of the continuum hypothesis'. Proceedings of the National Academy of Sciences of the United States of America, 50(6): 1143–8). *See also* THEOREMS. [HG]

Indiscernibility of Identicals. The indiscernibility of identicals is formally rendered thus: $(\forall x)(\forall y)(x=y \supset (Fx \equiv Fy))$. Informally, it is the claim that if, say, Jane is identical to Nancy, then whatever is true of Jane is true of Nancy and vice-versa. This seems obvious: if Jane and Nancy are not two different people but one person (who goes by two names) then it seems impossible for Jane to have a property Nancy lacks. Even so, there are some troublesome consequences of this principle. Here is one. Assume that Lois is unaware that mild-mannered Clark is actually flying superhero Superman. Accordingly, Lois believes (and will assert) that Superman can fly but Clark cannot. It seems to follow that Superman has a property that Clark lacks, viz. the property 'being thought by Lois to be able to fly'. But this contradicts the principle of the indiscernibility of identicals. If we accept that principle we must say either that Lois believes Clark can fly (something she will deny) or claim that a property like 'being thought by Lois to be able to fly' is, perhaps because it concerns the propositional attitudes, somehow not a genuine property. Neither option is free from problems of its own. *See also* IDENTITY; IDENTITY OF THE INDISCERNIBLES; PROPERTY; LEIBNIZ, GOTTFRIED WILHELM. [APM]

Induction. Induction is the form of reasoning where a thinker's premises provide her with good, yet not conclusive, reasons to believe her conclusions.

Having tasted lots of lemons I conclude that all lemons are bitter. I have good reason to think this, but this conclusion does not necessarily follow from the limited evidence that I have; the premisses could be true and the conclusion false. Induction leads to conclusions that are likely to be true, or that are probably true, rather than to ones that are certainly true. Such reasoning aims to extend our knowledge: the content of inductive conclusions goes beyond the content of the relevant premisses. A claim is made about all lemons from my experience of only some lemons. Induction can therefore involve arguments of different strengths: if I taste a million lemons, all bitter, I have more reason to think that all lemons are bitter than if I taste only ten. Such reasoning is contrasted with deduction: this involves the drawing of conclusions that must be true if the premisses are true; deductive conclusions are certain, not probable. Induction used to refer only to induction by enumeration, but the term now covers a wider range of non-deductive inferences. *See also* DEDUCTION; INDUCTION BY ENUMERATION; LOGIC, INDUCTIVE. [DOB]

Induction by Enumeration. Induction by enumeration is the simplest form of inductive reasoning. From the premise that all observed *F*s have been *G*, the conclusion is drawn that all *F*s are *G*. From the fact that all the peas I have seen have been green, I infer that all peas are green. There is also a probabilistic form of this kind of inference: from the premise that 1% of opened oysters have contained pearls, the conclusion is drawn that 1% of all oysters contain pearls. *See also* INDUCTION; LOGIC, INDUCTIVE. [DOB]

Inference. An inference is an action of drawing a conclusion from a set of premisses, data or evidence. A good or valid inference is such that its premisses justify its conclusion. While we have no general theory of what sets of premisses count as a justification for a conclusion, the special case of deductive inference is well understood. Validity in this case reduces to the ordinary notion of logical consequence which has been the primary business of logic since its inception. On the other hand we still lack a satisfying account of the validity of even more widespread inferences, especially inductive inferences. *See also* INDUCTION; INFERENCE, RULES OF; LOGICAL CONSEQUENCE; PREMISS; VALIDITY. [HG]

Inference to the Best Explanation. A method of reasoning, also known as *abduction*, in which the truth of an hypothesis is inferred on the grounds that it provides the best explanation of the relevant evidence. In general, inference to the best explanation (IBE) is an ampliative (i.e., non-deductive) method. In cases where *a* is not only the best explanation of *b* but *a* also entails *b* then IBE is formally equivalent to the logical fallacy of *affirming the consequent*. However, IBE does not license inferring *a* merely on the basis of the fact that *a* entails *b*. Criticisms of IBE come in both local and global varieties. Locally, such inferences are always defeasible because one can never be sure that all potential explanations have been found and hence that there is not some better, hitherto undiscovered explanation of the given evidence. Globally, some philosophers have questioned the grounds for taking explanatoriness as a guide to truth in the first place. There is also the practical issue of determining criteria for the comparison of different explanations, perhaps borrowing from more general criteria of theory choice such as simplicity, fruitfulness, expressive power and so on. There has been a tendency to see IBE as a distinctive feature of the empirical sciences. However, there are reasons for thinking that IBE may also play a role in the formal sciences, including both logic and mathematics, when it comes to choosing axioms. Thus a rationale for favouring one particular set of axioms may be that it provides the best explanation of the core results in the theory under scrutiny. *See also* ABDUCTION; AXIOM; FALLACY; INDUCTION. [ABa]

Inference, Rules of. Logical proofs are comprised of inference steps, which must conform to prevailing rules of inference. Typically, each rule specifies the logical form of the proposition(s) from which a proposition of a given form may be derived. Inference rules should be sound in the sense that they must not license invalid inferences. Where possible, proof systems are also expected to be 'complete': permitting the derivation of *all* valid inferences.

All proof systems include at least one inference rule. 'Hilbert-style' presentations contain only one rule, typically modus ponens, supplemented by axioms. However, Gerhard Gentzen's natural deduction presentations are comprised solely of inference rules. Natural deduction is so-called because it mimics the informal reasoning of practicing mathematicians, something axiomatic systems fail to do. Most modern textbook accounts of proof are descended from Gentzen's work.

Gentzen's version of natural deduction provides each connective with introduction and elimination rules, respectively, permitting the derivation of a proposition containing the connective from other propositions in which the connective need not appear, and vice-versa. Not all systems employ these 'intelim' rules exclusively. The influential presentation of Irving Copi (1961. *Introduction to Logic*, 2nd edition, New York: Macmillan.) includes the following rules:

Modus ponens: From a conditional and its antecedent, infer the consequent. That is,

φ→ψ, φ ∴ ψ

Modus tollens: From a conditional and the negation of its consequent, infer the negation of the antecedent. That is,

φ→ψ, ¬ψ ∴ ¬φ

Hypothetical syllogism: From two conditionals, such that the consequent of the former is the antecedent of the latter, infer a conditional having the antecedent of the former and the consequent of the latter. That is,

φ→ψ, ψ→ξ ∴ φ→ξ

Disjunctive syllogism: From a disjunction and the negation of one of the disjuncts, infer the other disjunct. That is,

φ∨ψ, ¬φ ∴ ψ

Constructive dilemma: From the conjunction of two conditionals and the disjunction of their antecedents, infer the disjunction of their consequents. That is,

(φ→ψ)∧(ξ→ζ), φ∨ξ ∴ ψ∨ζ

Absorption: From a conditional, infer a conditional with the same antecedent and the conjunction of antecedent and consequent as consequent. That is,

φ→ψ ∴ φ→(φ∧ψ)

Simplification: From a conjunction, infer one of its conjuncts. That is,

φ∧ψ ∴ φ

Conjunction: From two propositions, infer their conjunction. That is,

φ, ψ ∴ φ∧ψ

Addition: From a proposition, infer its disjunction with any proposition. That is,

φ ∴ φ∨ψ

Copi's conjunction and simplification are Gentzen's intelim rules for 'and', but some rules for the other connectives deviate from that plan. Copi thereby avoids rules, such as implication introduction, which refer back to the derivation of premises. This makes his system incomplete, a problem he remedies with a 'Rule of Replacement' permitting substitution of propositions by their logical equivalents.

As their Latin names suggest, many of Copi's rules predate natural deduction: several are from the Stoics. Natural deduction may be extended to predicate and modal logic by providing inference rules for quantifiers and modal operators. *See also* AXIOM; CONNECTIVES; PROOF THEORY; QUANTIFICATION RULES; SOUNDNESS; VALIDITY. [AA]

Intension. The intension of a property, a concept or a term *P* is the set of the features that an object has to have in order to characterize *P*, for example, the intension of 'red' is the set of the properties that characterize redness, like 'being a colour' or 'having a certain wave-length'. *See also* PROPERTY; SET; CARNAP, RUDOLF. [FB]

Interpretation. In the propositional calculus an interpretation is an assignment of truth-values to the atomic sentences of the language. It may be extended to all the sentences of the language through the truth-tables of the connectives. In the predicate logic an interpretation is an assignment of meaning from the variables and predicates of the language to the domain of discourse. In particular, an interpretation of first-order predicate logic consists of a domain of individuals and a function f of assignment, which correlates the individuals of the domain with first-order constants and classes of individuals to predicates. *See also* CONNECTIVES; DOMAIN; LOGIC, PREDICATE; MEANING; PREDICATE; PROPOSITIONAL CALCULUS; TRUTH-TABLE; TRUTH-VALUE; VARIABLE. [FB]

Intuitionism. Intuitionism is a school in the philosophy of mathematics founded by the Dutch mathematician L. E. J. Brouwer. According to Brouwer, mathematics is a creation of the mind: only mathematical objects that can actually be constructed can be said to exist. Brouwer grounded the existence of the natural numbers in our *intuition* of the movement of time: to the intuition of what once was corresponds the number 1; to the intuition of what once was and of what now is corresponds the intuition of the number 2; and so on. The truth of a mathematical statement is itself equated with the actual existence of a proof, in stark contrast with the realist view that the truth of a mathematical statement consists in its correspondence with an independent mathematical reality.

The so-called Brouwer-Heyting-Kolmogorov (BHK) clauses for the logical constants provide an informal characterization of the intuitionist notion of proof. The notion of a proof for atomic statements is taken as basic, and the proof-conditions of complex statements are defined in terms of the proof-conditions of their constituents. For the propositional case: a proof of a conjunction $A \wedge B$ is given by presenting a proof of A and a proof of B, a proof of $A \vee B$ is given by presenting either a proof of A or a proof of B, a proof of $A \rightarrow B$ is a construction that allow us to convert any proof of A into a proof of B; there is no proof of $\perp$ (where $\perp$ is a necessarily false proposition, for example $0 = 1$).

The BHK semantics validates intuitionistic, but not classical, logic. The Law of Excluded Middle fails, since for all we know, it is not the case that, for every statement, either it or its negation has a proof. Other notable casualties include Classical Reduction and Double Negation Elimination: from the fact that $\neg A$ has no proof, it does not follow that A itself has a proof. *See also* BIVALENCE; BROUWER'S PROGRAMME; CONNECTIVES; EXCLUDED MIDDLE, PRINCIPLE OF; PROOF THEORY; BROUWER, LUITZEN EGBERTUS JAN. [JM]

Invalidity. A structural flaw in the reasoning of a deductive argument. 'Invalid' means 'not valid'. To say that an argument is invalid is to say that its conclusion does not follow logically from its premise(s). This means: it's possible to make the premise(s) true and the conclusion false. Consider: '$A{\to}B$, B therefore A'. Its premisses can be true while the conclusion is false, so it is an invalid argument. Invalid arguments allow counterexamples. Though invalidity is typically undesirable, invalid arguments can still be worthwhile from an inductive point of view: the premises might still provide some support for the conclusion. Inductive arguments can be strong even while the possibility of making the premise(s) true and conclusion false remains. *See also* ARGUMENT; CONJUNCTION; COUNTEREXAMPLE; INDUCTION; LOGIC; VALIDITY. [CF]

Logic. In logic, we study arguments. An argument consists of a set of premisses together with a conclusion. For instance:

If you had measles, you would have a rash. You do not have a rash. Therefore, you do not have measles.

The first two sentences of this argument express its premisses; the third expresses its conclusion. In logic, we are interested in whether the premisses of such an argument support the truth of its conclusion. If the truth of its premisses guarantees the truth of its conclusion, we say that the argument is deductively valid. If it provides a weaker support, it is only inductively valid.

Aristotle inaugurated the study of deductive logic when he noticed that different arguments sometimes share the same form; and, what's more, they might all be deductively valid in virtue of sharing this form. For instance, the following argument shares the same form as the argument above:

If God were good, there would be no pain. There is pain. Therefore, God is not good.

We might write this shared form as follows.

If A, then B. It is not the case that B. Therefore, it is not the case that A.

Clearly, every argument that shares this form will be deductively valid, regardless of what A and B are, and regardless of whether or not they are in fact true.

So, if deductive logic explores the deductive validity of an argument by asking whether it is of a deductively valid form, can we enumerate all the deductively valid arguments by enumerating all the deductively valid forms? This is the project of deductive logic, and Aristotle thought he had completed it. He described 19 basic deductively valid forms of argument, and claimed that every deductively valid argument is made up of instances of these basic forms strung together.

Unfortunately, he was wrong for two reasons:

(1) There are deductively valid arguments that do not have the sort of form with which Aristotle deals.

(2) Among those arguments whose form is of that sort, there are valid arguments that cannot be written as a string of Aristotle's basic forms.

Deductive logic had to wait until 1879 to solve (2), and until 1930 to know it had been solved. In his *Begriffsschrift*, Gottlob Frege stated a recipe by which to produce deductively valid argument forms of the sort that Aristotle had considered; and, in his doctoral dissertation, Kurt Gödel showed that all deductively valid argument forms of that sort are generated by following this recipe.

However, (1) has been the concern of logic throughout the twentieth century. Many different sorts of argument forms have been identified: for instance, those studied in second-order, modal and deontic logic.

Furthermore, within the study of a particular sort of argument form, different notions of validity have been considered: as already mentioned, in inductive logic we seek arguments whose premisses provide a weaker sort of support to their conclusion. Research in this area strives after analogues to Frege's and Gödel's results about deductive logic. *See also* ARGUMENT; LOGICAL FORM VALIDITY; ARISTOTLE; FREGE, GOTTLOB; GÖDEL, KURT. [RP]

Logic and Games. Games are situations of strategic interaction. Game theory is an applied mathematical theory that studies strategies of players in such settings. Standard game theory identifies equilibria, that is, situations in which each player has adopted as a strategy a best response to his opponents. Epistemic game theory studies the role of players' beliefs and knowledge in games. There are close connections between the role of reasoning in game theory and logical reasoning, mirrored by the two ways in which logic and games connect:

Logic in Games. Logic helps to understand games by clarifying their logical structure, how the players reason about their opponents and what types of inferences they can use, for example counterfactuals. Logic can also improve game theory's analysis of the role of beliefs and knowledge in the players' reasoning. Different modal logics have been developed to formally model such problems, the most prominent being dynamic epistemic logic which builds on modal logic, epistemic logic and AGM belief revision to provide a logic of change of information and knowledge (van Ditmarsch et al. 2008: *Dynamic Epistemic Logic*, Springer).

Games in Logic. Logicians use so-called evaluation games to determine truth-values of sentences in game semantics. In such evaluation games, a semantic tree is interpreted as a dynamic game with perfect information between a 'verifier' and a 'falsifier'. A formula is true if and only if the verifier has a winning strategy. Games are also used in proof theory and model-theoretic games are employed in the foundations of mathematics, for example, in forcing (Hodges, Wilfrid. 2003. 'Logic and Games', *The Stanford Encyclopedia of Philosophy*. Springer). *See also* AGM; FORCING; FOUNDATIONS OF MATHEMATICS; LOGIC; LOGIC, EPISTEMIC; LOGIC, NORMAL-MODAL; PROOF THEORY; SEMANTIC TREE. [CH]

Logic Programming. A style of programming based on first-order logic, generally used for artificial intelligence and computational linguistics. The best-known logic programming language is Prolog. A logic program consists of a database of clauses, which can be facts or rules. An example of a fact is 'Socrates is human', which can be written in Prolog as *human (Socrates)*. An example of a rule is 'All humans are mortal', which becomes *mortal(X):- human(X).* in Prolog. After supplying the logic programming system with a database, the user asks the system to prove a goal, for example *mortal (Socrates),* in Prolog. The system then attempts to prove the goal by resolution and recursively breaking it down into subgoals and trying to prove them until it reaches facts in the database. A fact is a goal without subgoals, so it is always true. Prolog combines this recursive way of proving the goal with backtracking: if it can prove the first subgoal and then cannot prove the other subgoals based on the solution of the first subgoal, the system 'backtracks' and tries the next possible solution to the first subgoal. Backtracking terminates when there are no more solutions of the first subgoal. A clause can contain variables such as '*X*' in our example. In the resolution step, this variable can take the value of the logical constant it is matched to, such as 'Socrates'. Logic programming has also been extended with higher order programming features derived from higher order logic, such as predicate variables appearing in quantifications. *See also* CLOSED WORLD ASSUMPTION; LOGIC; NEGATION AS FAILURE; RESOLUTION. [KV]

Logic vs Linguistics. Linguistics often incorporates logic to explain natural language understanding, but logic is independent, and sometimes at odds with, natural language data. Consider S ='no one loves no one'. This can mean *everyone is a lover*, $\neg(\exists x)\neg(\exists y)Lxy$, but linguists observe that speakers don't interpret S as *everyone is loved* (= *no one* no one loves), ¬(∃y)¬(∃x)Lxy, which is an equally possible logical interpretation. Further, speakers detect scope differences between 'everyone loves someone', (∀y)(∃x)Lyx, and 'someone (say, Ervin), everyone loves', (∃x)(∀y)Lyx, but detect no scope dominance in S's 'easiest' reading, *no one is a lover*, even though logic assigns a dominant quantifier in its representation. (Branching quantifiers address this issue.) *See also* SCOPE. [ABr]

Logic, Algebraic. Symbolic logic was invented as an algebra by George Boole. An algebra is a set closed under some finitary operations. The set of well-formed formulae of a propositional logic comprises its word algebra. The Lindenbaum algebra of a logic is the quotient of the word algebra by a congruence relation, which is defined by mutual provability between formulae. For example, $A \wedge B$ and $B \wedge A$ are two formulae that are equivalent, and they can replace each other in any formula, hence they are elements of the same equivalence class in the Lindenbaum algebra.

The algebra of classical logic is a Boolean algebra, whereas nonclassical logics algebraize into a Heyting algebra, a De Morgan monoid, a residuated monoid, various modal algebras, a BCI algebra, a Kleene algebra etc. (The prototypical Boolean algebras are power sets with intersection, union and complementation.) The Lindenbaum algebra facilitates the definition of various semantics (e.g. relational, operational and algebraic semantics), and sometimes it allows results from universal algebra to be applied.

Quantification may be treated algebraically too, for example, classical predicate logic can be dealt with using Tarski's cylindric algebras or Halmos' polyadic algebras. The algebraic approach straightforwardly generalizes into a category theoretic view of logics. *See also* INTUITIONISM; LOGIC, PREDICATE; LOGIC, PROPOSITIONAL; LOGIC, RELEVANT; SEMANTICS; BOOLE, GEORGE; DE MORGAN, AUGUSTUS; LINDENBAUM, ADOLF. [KB]

Logic, Deontic. Deontic logic concerns obligation and permissibility. By adapting the modal logic K, we obtain D, an elementary standard deontic logic, as follows. Replace K's necessity operator with 'O' (interpreted as 'It is obligatory that . . . ') and its possibility operator with 'P' (interpreted as 'It is permissible that . . . '). To the thus amended K axioms, add axiom (D): $O\varphi \rightarrow P\varphi$, which expresses the ethical principle that whatever is obligatory is permissible. *See also* AXIOM; LOGIC, NORMAL-MODAL; LOGICAL OPERATOR; NECESSITY. [SML]

Logic, Doxastic. Doxastic logic, beginning with Hintikka's *Knowledge and Belief. An Introduction to the Logic of the Two Notions* (1962. Cornell University Press), studies relations between propositions about what we believe. Using 'a' as a proper name like 'Ann', '→' for 'if' as opposed to material implication, propositional variables such as 'p', 'q' and 'B' to represent the two-place relation, ' . . . believes that . . . '.

Ann believes that it is raining.

is formalized:

Bap.

Uncontroversial is,

Ba(p & q) → (Bap & Baq).

Controversial, even for ideally rational believers, are so-called 'BB' principles:

Bap → BaBap

and conversely. *See also* LOGIC, EPISTEMIC; LOGIC, NORMAL-MODAL; MATERIAL EQUIVALENCE; PROPOSITION; PROPOSITIONAL VARIABLE. [JW]

Logic, Dynamic. Dynamic logic is a branch of nonclassical logic which includes dynamic versions of propositional, modal, and predicate logics. Each state is a classical model with a static assignment of truth-values to propositions or objects to sets. Dynamic logics can express the change of these assignments that occurs while moving between states. They are used for modelling phenomena such as action, knowledge, and belief change (van Ditmarsch et al. 2008. *Dynamic Epistemic Logic*, Springer), and computer programmes (Fischer et al. 1979. Propositional dynamic logic of regular programs. *Journal of Computer and System Sciences*, 18: 194–211.). *See also* AGM; LOGIC, DEONTIC; LOGIC, DOXASTIC; LOGIC, EPISTEMIC; LOGIC, NORMAL-MODAL; LOGIC, PROPOSITIONAL; LOGIC, PREDICATE; SET; TRUTH-VALUE. [SU]

Logic, Epistemic. Epistemic logic is the branch of modal logic concerned with knowledge and belief.

Let a be an arbitrary agent. The underlining idea of epistemic logic is to use the box modality '□' to translate, in a formal modal logic, a's epistemic propositional attitudes, that is, attitudes such as 'a believes that . . . ' and 'a knows that . . . '. If A is the proposition that the sky is blue, then the intuitive interpretation of the expression '□A' is 'a believes / knows that the sky is blue'. Given this translation, one can then characterize various conceptions of belief / knowledge by specifying the modal principles that '□' satisfies.

Epistemic logic assumes agents are logically omniscient, this means that (1) they know all logical truths and (2) they know the logical consequences of what they know. Formally, these assumptions correspond to the conditions:

(Nec) If ϕ is a logical truth then $\Box\phi$

and

(K) $\Box(\phi \to \psi) \to (\Box\phi \to \Box\psi)$,

which make epistemic logic (at least) a minimal modal logic **K**. Adding the requirement that an agent's beliefs be consistent corresponds to adding the condition

(D) $\Box\phi \to \neg\Box\neg\phi$,

stating that everything that is known is not known to be false. The property that distinguishes knowledge from belief is usually taken to be truth, which corresponds to the condition

(T) $\Box\phi \to \phi$,

that is, all that is known is true. Some 'higher order' conditions are often required of knowledge: first, one may want everything that is known to be known to be known:

(4) $\Box\phi \to \Box\phi$,

and second, that all that is unknown be known to be such:

(5) $\neg\Box\phi \rightarrow \Box\neg\Box\phi$.

The most prominent axiomatizations of knowledge are **S4** (K+T+4) and **S5** (K+T+4+5).

An epistemic interpretation of the Kripke semantics for these modal logics can also be given. Possible worlds are viewed as epistemic or conceivable alternatives, and the accessibility relation between worlds is understood as follows: *v* is accessible from *w* if, from the agent's perspective (or, for all the agent knows), *v* can't be distinguished from *w*. *See also* LOGIC, NORMAL-MODAL; POSSIBLE WORLD. [NK]

Logic, Erotetic. Erotetic logic is the logic of questions and answers. Given a question Q, erotetic logic studies, for instance, when a proposition answers Q, what is a presupposition of Q and when Q implies another question Q'. For a survey, *see* D. Harrah, "The logic of questions", in Gabbay and Guenthner (eds.), Handbook of Philosophical Logic, Kluwer, 2002. *See also* LOGIC, EPISTEMIC; LOGIC, PREDICATE. [GC]

Logic, Fuzzy. Vagueness concerns cases where it is not possible to provide absolute characterizations for objects, properties etc. For example, when someone is 60 years old, she is not absolutely old but old to a degree. Fuzziness is a special form of vagueness which is based on the idea that some element belongs to a set with some degree, which is usually a (real) number between zero and one. A set having this property is called a *fuzzy set* and the accompanying logic is called *fuzzy logic*. Since elements belong to some degree to a fuzzy set, fuzzy propositions are not just either true or false. In the simplest case, a fuzzy proposition may assume a truth-value which is an element of the unit interval (i.e., of the set of all real numbers that belong to [0,1]). For example, we could say that Mary, who is 30 years old, is old to a degree which is equal to 0.20. Fuzzy logic is an *infinite-valued* logic, since the unit interval contains an infinite number of elements. Assume that *p* and *q* are two fuzzy propositions. Also, assume that *T(p)* and *T(q)* denote the truth-value of the corresponding propositions. Then the following equations define the truth-values of the basic logical operations.

$T(\neg p) = 1 - T(p)$
$T(p \lor q) = \max \{T(p), T(q)\}$
$T(p \land q) = \min \{T(p), T(q)\}$

Fuzzy implication is defined by using the formula $\neg p \lor q$ as follows:

$T(p \Rightarrow q) = \max \{1 - T(p), T(q)\}.$

Similarly, one can define other logical operators. In the previous equations, we have used the operators max and min to define the corresponding logical operators. It is quite possible to replace these operators with others that are called t-norms and t-conorms, respectively, This way, one can define a class of logics. Fuzzy logic has been extensively used in computer systems that model and/or simulate real-life systems. For example, fuzzy logic has been used in industrial applications and even in spacecraft landing-site selection on planets. *See also* LOGIC, MULTI-VALUED; PROPOSITION; SET. [AS]

Logic, Inductive. Inductive logic takes various forms, and the simplest characterization of what these have in common is that they involve inference that is not deductive. Inductive inferences are contingent, that is, the conclusions of inductive arguments do not necessarily follow from the premisses; there is no guarantee that true premisses lead to true inductive conclusions. Rather, the conclusions are plausible given the premisses. Some inductive inferences draw general conclusions from particular cases: from the premise that all emeralds in my experience have been green, I draw the conclusion that all emeralds are green. Conversely, some draw particular conclusions from general claims: from the premise that all previous raindrops were wet, the conclusion is drawn that the next raindrop will be wet. And some draw particular conclusions from particular cases: from the premise that this ice cube is cold, and this one, and this one, it is concluded that the one over there is also cold. Inference to the best explanation and analogy are commonly used forms of inductive inference.

David Hume argued that inductive inference is not valid, and that there is no reason at all to think the conclusions of such arguments are true; we cannot even say that our inductive conclusions are probably true. Hume claimed that inductive inference is just something that creatures like us find it natural to do, even though it has no logical justification. There is no deductive reason to think that inductive inference is valid – no guarantee that inductive conclusions follow from their premises – and so the only way to justify induction is non-deductively or inductively, but this would be to reason in a circle. Induction depends on the assumption that I have experienced a representative sample of reality, that my limited experience of Fs is likely to lead to true conclusions concerning all Fs. But what reason have I to think that this is true? My experience may have been a good guide so far, but to think that it will continue to be so would be to assume that induction is valid, and this begs the question against the Humean sceptic.

Various responses have been offered to the Problem of Induction. Karl Popper accepted that induction is not justified but argued that this is not important because in both everyday reasoning and science we use a form of deductive reasoning instead. In contrast, several attempts have been made to justify induction. It has been argued that inductive inference is by definition rational and thus justified; that if any form of reasoning can identify regularities in nature, induction can, and thus inductive inference is pragmatically justified; and, even though an argument cannot be provided to justify induction, it turns out that inductive inference is reliable – it leads to true conclusions – and thus, again, such reasoning is justified. There is, however, no consensus on whether any of these strategies are successful. *See also* ANALOGY; DEDUCTION; INDUCTION BY ENUMERATION; INFERENCE TO THE BEST EXPLANATION. [DOB]

Logic, Intuitionistic. *See* INTUITIONISM.

Logic, Linear. Linear logic is a resource conscious logic. In classical and intuitionistic logic a premise can be used any number of times – linear logic doesn't assume this. Linear logic tracks the number of times a formula is used in an argument – each premise must be used exactly once. While the argument $A \therefore A$ is valid, $A, B \therefore A$ is not (thus linear logic is a substructural logic). Suppose that $A, A \therefore B$ is a valid argument, it doesn't follow that $A \therefore B$ is. Linear logic aims to neither lose nor add information in the transition from premisses to conclusion.

Linear logic does not only consider how many times a formula is used, it also considers in what manner information is extracted from a formula.

Suppose that $A \therefore C$ is a valid argument. Should *A and B* $\therefore C$ be valid (the argument with the single premise *A and B* and conclusion C)? *A and B* can be used once to conclude *A* and then *A* can be used to conclude *C*; so the argument seems good. However, there is more information that can be extracted from *A and B*; namely, that *B* is true. Linear logic has two conjunctions! The information *A* and the information *B* can be extracted from the conjunction *A & B*, but not both in a single use of *A & B*. If *A* ∴ *C* is valid then so is *A & B* ∴ *C*. The conjunction *A ⊗ B* justifies *A* and justifies *B*, but unlike the first conjunction, this occurs in a single use of the conjunction. The argument *A ⊗ B* ∴ *C* is valid if and only if *A, B* ∴ *C* is (comma separates the premises of the argument). There are also two different disjunctions.

Linear logic does not attempt to replace classical and intuitionistic logic, but to extend it by exposing the structure within these logics. The operators ! and ? (called exponentials) are used to reintroduce the propositions of classical and intuitionistic logic. The formula !*A* contains the information *A* does but can be used as many times as one likes. In this way !*A* acts like *A* does in other logics. ?*A* performs the same role with the conclusions of arguments as !*A* does for premises. The exponentials can be used to give a structured translation of classical and intuitionistic logic into linear logic. *See also* ARGUMENT; CONNECTIVES; PREMISS; LOGIC, INTUITIONISTIC; LOGIC, RELEVANT; LOGIC, SUBSTRUCTURAL; VALIDITY. [CA]

Logic, Multi-valued. Multivalued logics generalize classical logic by admitting of more than the usual two truth-values, usual examples ranging from three (Kleene's K_3 or Priest's *LP*) to a continuum of values (Fuzzy logic). Some truth-values are distinguished as 'designated' and used to extend the notion of logical consequence: *A* is a logical consequence of Γ if and only if, for all interpretations, if the premises have designated truth-values, so has the conclusion. Notice that a mere difference in the set of designated values makes for very different logics, as shown by a comparison between for example *LP* (two designated values and a paraconsistent logic) and K_3 (one designated value and not paraconsistent). *See also* LOGIC, FUZZY; LOGIC, PARACONSISTENT; LOGICAL CONSEQUENCE; MODEL. [HG]

Logic, Nonmonotonic. In classical logic, the conclusion of a valid argument must be true if all of the premises are. Adding additional premises to the argument, therefore, will never cause a valid argument to become invalid: if 'Φ' is a logical consequence of a set of premises Γ and Δ results from adding extra premises to Γ (i.e., Γ⊆Δ), then 'Φ' must be a logical consequence of Δ, too. This property is known as monotonicity and any notion of logical consequence with this feature is said to be a monotonic consequence relation.

Many of the day-to-day inferences we make, however, are not monotonic. One might initially conclude that all swans are white but then, on seeing a black swan, withdraw the conclusion. The initial conclusion, based on the premises 'this swan here is white', 'that one there is white' and so on, was drawn nonmonotonically, for after the addition of the extra premise 'this swan isn't white', the argument no longer supports the conclusion. In a similar way, the police might draw the conclusion that Smith is the culprit, based on the evidence available at the time, but later, in light of new evidence, withdraw that tentative conclusion.

The initial conclusions drawn in these cases are defeasible: they may later be shown to be false. Defeasible reasoning also arises when we use the closed world assumption, that is, the assumption that the information we have is all the relevant information. If a library catalogue does not contain a record for 'Key Terms in Logic', one concludes that the library does not have a copy. But the catalogue might be incomplete, so the conclusion is not guaranteed to be true. Making the closed world assumption is nevertheless often valuable (it excuses us from an exhaustive search of the library's shelves, for example).

These examples of defeasible reasoning highlight just how common nonmonotonic inference is. If we were banned from drawing defeasible conclusions, we would be able to do very little practical reasoning at all. Nonmonotonic logics try to capture patterns of defeasible inference such as these, by allowing conclusions to follow from a set of premises even if those premises do not guarantee the truth of the conclusion. Typically, a nonmonotonic consequence relation is defined in terms of the classical consequence relation plus a number of additional default assumptions or rules, which are allowed to generate extra consequences provided that those consequences are consistent with the premises. As there are many possible ways of doing this, there are many possible nonmonotonic consequence relations.

By way of example, we can think of the closed world assumption as a set of default assumptions, each saying that the library doesn't contain a particular book. If the library's catalogue says that the library does contain that book, the corresponding default assumption may not be used. But for any book not mentioned by the catalogue, the corresponding assumption may be used and the conclusion that the book isn't in the library may be drawn. *See also* ABDUCTION; CLOSED WORLD ASSUMPTION; INDUCTION; LOGICAL CONSEQUENCE. [MJ]

Logic, N-Order. By n-order logic, we mean a formal system in which it is possible to quantify on n-order variables. First-order predicate calculus admits quantification on first order variables (interpreted on a domain of individuals). It is possible to provide more powerful logical systems allowing quantification on higher order variables. These are usually interpreted on sets (sets of individuals, sets of sets of individuals and so on) or on properties intensionally defined. It can be proven that every n-order ($n > 2$) logic can be reduced to second-order logic; the latter system, if interpreted through standard semantics, has remarkable expressive power. *See also* LOGIC, PREDICATE; LOGICAL CONSEQUENCE; SET THEORY. [CDF]

Logic, Normal-Modal. In a normal modal logic, L, (i) every tautology of propositional logic is L-valid; (ii) if $\vdash_L \varphi$ and $\vdash_L \varphi \rightarrow \phi$, then $\vdash_L \phi$ (closure under modus ponens); (iii) if $\vdash_L \varphi$ then $\vdash_L \Box\varphi$ (closure under necessitation); (iv) $\vdash_L \Box(\varphi \rightarrow \phi) \rightarrow (\Box\varphi \rightarrow \Box\phi)$ (axiom (K)). The system K (the weakest normal modal logic) and its extensions (e.g. T, D, B, S4 and S5) constitute the normal modal logics. *See also* AXIOM; LOGIC, PROPOSITIONAL; MODUS PONENS; TAUTOLOGY; THEOREM; VALIDITY. [SML]

Logic, Paraconsistent. In classical logic, every sentence is entailed by a contradiction: 'φ' and '$\neg\varphi$' together entail 'ψ', for any sentences 'φ' and 'ψ' whatsoever. This principle is often known as 'ex contradictione sequitur quodlibet' (from a contradiction, everything follows), or as the principle of explosion. In paraconsistent logic, by contrast, this principle does not hold (and so paraconsistent logics are contradiction tolerant). Although there are different approaches to paraconsistent logic, one of the most popular makes use of a valuation relation V between sentences and truth-values, rather than the usual valuation function. V can relate each sentence to either true, or to false, or to both (an alternative is to introduce a third truth-value, both true and false). V evaluates logically complex sentences as follows:

$V (\neg\varphi, \textbf{true})$ iff $V (\varphi, \textbf{false})$

$V (\neg\varphi, \textbf{false})$ iff $V (\varphi, \textbf{true})$

$V(\varphi \wedge \psi, \textbf{true})$ iff $V(\varphi, \textbf{true})$ and $V(\psi, \textbf{true})$
$V(\varphi \wedge \psi, \textbf{false})$ iff $V(\varphi, \textbf{false})$ and $V(\psi, \textbf{false})$

and so on for the other connectives. This approach gives Asenjo's Logic of Paradox, **LP** Surprisingly, the validities of **LP** (true under every such V) are exactly the classical tautologies. But modus ponens is not valid in **LP**, for both 'φ' and '$\varphi \to \psi$' can be true while 'ψ' is not true.

There are both practical and philosophical motivations for paraconsistent logic. A practical application is reasoning with inconsistent information, for example automated reasoning in large databases. Using paraconsistent logic does not force one to admit that contradictions could be true, but only that we sometimes need to draw sensible conclusions from inconsistent data. Some philosophers, including Richard Sylvan and Graham Priest, believe that there are true contradictions and so are known as 'dialethists'. They cite the liar sentence, 'this sentence is not true' which, if true, is false and, if false, is true and so looks to be a true contradiction. As dialethists do not want to say that a true contradiction entails everything, they adopt a paraconsistent logic. *See also* CONTRADICTION; LOGIC, MULTI-VALUED; LOGIC, RELEVANT; PARADOX; TRUTH-VALUE. [MJ]

Logic, Predicate. Predicate logic is the formal calculus that extends propositional logic by representing the internal structure of what in propositional logic appear as basic elements, that is, of propositions. Consider the following valid argument:

All men are mortal.
Socrates is a man.
Therefore, Socrates is mortal.

Upon translation into propositional logic, this yields:

A
B
Therefore, C

This is invalid: given A and B, nothing forces us to believe that C is the case.

To express the above inference, we need to be able to talk about individuals and their properties, which is what predicate logic does.

In addition to the logical symbols of propositional logic ($\neg$, $\wedge$, $\vee$, $\rightarrow$, $\leftrightarrow$), predicate logic makes use of: variables (x, y, . . .) and constants (a, b, . . .) denoting individuals; properties and relation symbols (P, R, . . . : for instance, '$P(c)$' says that individual c has property P, and '$R(a, b)$' expresses the fact that individuals a and b – in that order – stand in relation R); and quantifiers. The identity relation may or may not appear as a primitive in a predicate calculus.

Quantifiers, in particular, are an essential feature of predicate logic: they are the constructs that allow one to express information about the elements in the domain on the basis of their characteristics. Quantifiers specify the range of individuals which individual variables refer to. The two essential quantifiers (there are others) are the existential quantifier '$\exists$' ('there is one . . . ') and the universal quantifier '$\forall$' ('All . . . ').

First-order logic has individuals as the entities that are quantified over. Second-order logic quantifies over sets of individuals, that is, over first-order properties (since properties can be defined by pointing to the sets of entities sharing a certain feature). Since one can similarly quantify over sets of sets of individuals, sets of sets of sets of individuals and so on, there can be predicate logics of any order. In informal usage, however, predicate logic usually refers to first-order logic.

Getting back to predicate logic as a system of deduction, the above inference can be formalized as,

$\forall x(H(x) \rightarrow M(x))$
$H(s)$
Therefore, $M(s)$

where 'H' denotes the property of being a man, 'M' the property of being mortal and 's' stands for Socrates. So formalized, the inference can indeed be shown to be valid by employing the inference rules of predicate logic.

Predicate logic adds to the inference rules of propositional logic four new ones: universal instantiation, universal generalization, existential instantiation and existential generalization. The definition of the domain and of what the extra-logical symbols (constants, predicates and relations) mean in that domain constitutes an interpretation. A sentence in a predicate language is satisfiable if there exists an interpretation that makes it true (those sentences true in every interpretation of the language are logical truths); a model for a set of sentences in a first-order language is an interpretation that makes all those sentences true; consequently, consistency is the property of having a model; and deductive validity the property of being such that the set constituted by the premises and the negation of the consequence has no model. It is easy to see that, in our example, the set of sentences $\{\forall x(H(x)\rightarrow M(x)),\ H(s),\ \neg M(s)\}$ has no model.

Importantly, first-order predicate logic is complete and sound. Gödel's completeness theorem (1929) says that the inference rules of first-order predicate calculus are 'complete' in the sense that no additional inference rule is required to prove all the logically valid well-formed formulae of the language. This establishes a correspondence between semantic truth and syntactic provability in first-order logic. The converse fact that first-order predicate calculus is sound, that is, that only logically valid statements can be proven in first-order logic, is asserted by the soundness theorem.

Russell and Whitehead showed that predicate logic is sufficient for providing logical demonstrations of simple arithmetical truths. Gödel, however, demonstrated that (i) for any consistent formal theory that proves basic arithmetical truths, an arithmetical statement that is true but not provable in the theory can be constructed; (ii) for any formal theory T including basic arithmetical truths and also certain truths about formal provability, T includes a statement of its own consistency if and only if T is inconsistent – that is, any theory capable of expressing elementary arithmetic cannot be both consistent and complete. These are Gödel's celebrated incompleteness theorems (1931). *See also* ARGUMENT; DOMAIN; EXISTENTIAL QUANTIFIER; INFERENCE; INTERPRETATION; LOGIC, PROPOSITIONAL; MODEL; PROPERTY; QUANTIFIER; SOUNDNESS; THEOREMS; UNIVERSAL QUANTIFIER; VALIDITY; VARIABLE; GÖDEL, KURT; RUSSELL, BERTRAND; WHITEHEAD, ALFRED NORTH. [MMo]

Logic, Probabilistic. An extension of propositional logic that allows for probabilistic entailment among propositions. In propositional logic, logical relations are an either/or affair: for two propositions A and B, either A entails B, B entails A or neither entails the other. However, various thinkers (notably Keynes and Carnap) considered this too limited; they thought that a set of propositions can also give partial support to another proposition. For example, the proposition 'All cars are either red or green' might be seen to partially support the proposition that 'Your car is red', even though it does not strictly entail it. Probabilistic logic attempts to make this more precise.

It does this by interpreting the probability axioms – that is, the mathematical statements defining what a probability function is (e.g. that all probabilities take on values between 0 and 1) – as describing degrees of entailment between various (sets of) propositions. So, if, for two propositions A and B, it turned out that $p(A|B)=3/4$ (i.e., the probability of A given B is 3/4), then that can be interpreted as expressing the fact that proposition B partially entails A to degree 3/4. If no specific entailing proposition is specified, our background knowledge is to be used instead: for example, $p(A)=1/3$ expresses the fact that our background knowledge entails A to degree 1/3.

If successful, the major benefit of this approach would be that it can capture all that propositional logic can capture and some more besides. This is because it is possible to fully represent propositional logic in a probabilistic framework: the standard logical relations are just limiting cases of probabilistic relations (see e.g. Jaynes, E.T. 2003. *Probability Theory: The Logic of Science.* Cambridge University Press). For example, A entailing B turns out to be equivalent to $p(A|B)=1$, and A and B entailing $(A \wedge B)$ to be derivable from the fact that, if $p(A)=1$ and $p(B)=1$, it must also be the case that $p(A \wedge B)=1$.

On top of this, though, probabilistic logic also has available all the relations of partial entailment represented by probabilities between 0 and 1. For example, if we know that $p(A \wedge B)=1/2$ and $p(B)=3/4$, we can infer (using standard probabilistic reasoning) that $p(A|B)=2/3$. In other words, probabilistic logic makes clear that B must entail A to degree 2/3 if our background knowledge entails $(A \wedge B)$ to degree 1/2 and B to degree 3/4. In this way, the reach of traditional logic can be considerably widened.

Unfortunately, the approach also faces some difficulties. The most well-known of these concerns the fact that it is not clear how to determine the exact degree to which our background knowledge entails some proposition. Attempts have been made to use the 'Principle of Indifference' to achieve this; according to this principle, similarly structured propositions ought to be given the same probability. However, these attempts have not been successful as yet – mainly because it is not clear when, exactly, two propositions are 'similarly structured'. If this difficulty could be dealt with, though, probabilistic logic would be in a great position to fruitfully extend propositional logic. See also LOGIC; LOGIC, PROPOSITIONAL; PROBABILITY; PROPOSITION; CARNAP, RUDOLF. [AWS]

Logic, Propositional. Propositional logic deals with arguments whose validity depends only on the meaning of such words as 'and', 'or', 'not', 'if', 'then'. For example the validity of the argument 'if Peter is employed then Peter earns, Peter does not earn; therefore Peter is not employed' does not depend on the meaning of the words 'Peter', 'employed' and 'earn'. One can substitute these words with, respectively, 'John', 'French' and 'sing', and the resulting argument is still valid. The logical form of this argument is 'if A then B, not-B; thus not-A'. The letters A and B stand for sentences and are called propositional variables; the words 'or', 'and' and 'not' are called logical connectives.

Propositional variables, connectives and auxiliary symbols (such as parentheses) are the basic elements of the language of propositional logic. Propositional variables are the letters A, B, C, . . . ; connectives are the symbol $\neg$ (not), $\vee$ (or), $\wedge$ (and), $\rightarrow$ (if . . . then). Sentences are represented in propositional logic by strings of symbols called formulae. The definition of a formula is given in two steps:

1. Every propositional variable is a formula (called an atomic formula).
2. If A and B are formulae then $\neg(A)$, $(A \vee B)$, $(A \wedge B)$ and $(A \rightarrow B)$ are formulae; they respectively abbreviate 'not-A', 'A or B', 'A and B' and 'if A then B'.

Parentheses are frequently omitted when ambiguity is easily avoidable. Propositional logic makes use of axioms and inference rules in order to deduce consequences from axioms or from previously deduced statements. A proof of a formula F from the set S of premisses is a succession of formulae such that every formula is an axiom, or is in the set S, or is derivable from previous formulae by an inference rule.

There are several versions of propositional logic, which differ in axioms and inference rules. In classical propositional logic there are only two truth-values, true and false, and two laws hold: the law of the excluded middle ($A \vee \neg A$) and the law of double negation ($\neg A) \rightarrow A$. Intuitionistic propositional logic rejects both the law of the excluded middle and the law of double negation, although it recognizes only the two truth-values: true and false. Multi-valued logic recognizes more than two truth-values, for example true, false and indeterminate, or even an infinite number of truth-values. Even in classical propositional logic there are different ways for formulating axioms and rules or inference.

Connectives are truth-functional, that is the truth-value of every formula is a function of the truth-value of the constituent formulae. For example, the formula $(A \lor B)$ is false only when A and B are both false, independently of the meaning of A and B. A formula is called a tautology when it is true for every truth-value assignment to its atomic formula. Examples of tautologies of classical propositional logic are $(A \lor \neg A)$, $\neg(\neg A) \to A$ and $\neg(A \land \neg A)$. Formulae that are false for every truth-value assignment are called contradictions. Formulae that are neither tautologies nor contradictions are called contingent.

Starting from the four connectives $\neg$ (not), $\lor$ (or), $\land$ (and), $\to$ (if . . . then), it is possible to define other connectives. For example, the connective $\leftrightarrow$ (if and only if) can be defined so that the formula $(A \leftrightarrow B)$ is equivalent, by definition, to $(A \to B) \land (B \to A)$. Every connective is definable using only the four connectives $\neg$, $\lor$, $\land$, $\to$. (In fact, every connective is definable using $\neg$ and only one of the other three connectives.) Thus we say that classical propositional logic is functionally complete.

By definition, a set S of formulae entails a formula F when F is true whenever all formulae in S are true. There is an interesting relation between entailment and proof: If a formula F is provable from a set S of formulae then S entails F, and if S entails F then there exists a proof of F from the premises in S.

Other important properties concerning classical propositional logic are the following: If a formula F is provable then F is a tautology (soundness of propositional logic). If a formula F is a tautology then F is provable (completeness of propositional logic), and there exists a method that determines, for every formula F, whether F is a tautology (decidability of propositional logic). *See also* ARGUMENT; AXIOM; CONNECTIVES; DECIDABILITY; INFERENCE, RULES OF; INTUITIONISM; LOGIC, PREDICATE; MEANING; PROOF-THEORY; PROPOSITIONAL VARIABLE; SOUNDNESS; TRUTH-TABLES; VALIDITY. [MMu]

Logic, Quantum. Quantum logics are logical systems inspired by quantum mechanics. Several quite different approaches have been proposed, but the earliest and best known is that of Garrett Birkhoff and John von Neumann (1936. The logic of quantum mechanics. *Annals of Mathematics*, 37: 823–43). They exploited a similarity between the standard mathematical presentation of quantum mechanics and the structure of propositional logic. In the former, observations performed on a quantum-mechanical system correspond to subspaces of a certain sort of vector space, known as a Hilbert space. Various operations on these subspaces are more or less analogous to the connectives 'and', 'or' and 'not.' Some of the operations depend on concepts alien to orthodox logic, such as orthogonality, which may throw doubt on whether the resultant system truly is a logic. Implication may be introduced by definition, and quantifiers by analogy with conjunction and disjunction.

Quantum logic differs in various respects from classical logic. Crucially, it is non-distributive: $A \wedge (B \vee C) \nvdash (A \wedge B) \vee (A \wedge C)$ in all practical cases. This preserves a well-known idiosyncrasy of quantum mechanics: that the position and momentum of a particle may not be simultaneously measured. For a particle could have a known momentum, and one of some finite range of positions, but in quantum logic the distributive law could not be used to infer that it must have that momentum and the first position, or that momentum and the second position, or any other such combination, each of which corresponds to an impossible observation.

Birkhoff and von Neumann did not suggest that quantum logic should replace classical logic, nor that it resolves the anomalies of quantum mechanics. Both positions were strenuously defended by Hilary Putnam (1969. Is logic empirical?, reprinted in his *Mathematics, Matter and Method*. Cambridge: Cambridge University Press, 174–97), although he subsequently recanted. More philosophically modest research continues. *See also* LOGIC, ALGEBRAIC; CONNECTIVES; IMPLICATION. [AA]

Logic, Relevant. Relevant logics (also known as 'relevance logics') are a group of logics which do not allow irrelevant conclusions to be drawn from a set of premisses. In classical logic, the inference from 'logic is useful' to 'either the moon is made of green cheese or it isn't' is valid, for there is no way in which the premise can be true but the conclusion false. But there is something suspect about calling such inferences acceptable, for the premise is utterly irrelevant to the conclusion. If we let 'Φ' and 'ψ' be any two sentences, the following inferences are all valid in classical logic:

- from 'ϕ', one may infer '$\psi \to \phi$', '$\psi \to \psi$' and '$\psi \vee \neg \psi$';
- from '$\neg \phi$', one may infer '$\phi \to \psi$'; and
- from '$\phi \wedge \neg \phi$', one may infer 'ψ'.

But if 'Φ' and 'ψ' are utterly irrelevant to one another, we feel reluctant to call these inferences acceptable. Each classically valid inference from 'Φ' to 'ψ'

can be re-written as a valid material implication, '$\phi \to \psi$' (defined as '$\neg\Phi \lor \Psi$'). These 'paradoxes' of material implication highlight the difficulty in translating 'if . . . then' using the material conditional.

Most relevant logics insist that an inference is valid only if the premisses and the conclusion have at least one propositional variable in common. Given this principle, the classically valid inference from '$A \land \neg A$' to 'B' is not valid in relevant logic, because 'B' does not appear in the premisses and 'A' does not appear in the conclusion. Note that this variable-sharing condition does not rule out the inference from 'A' to '$B \to A$', or from '$\neg A$' to '$A \to B$' and so it is a necessary but not a sufficient condition for an entailment to be acceptable in relevant logic. Relevant logic should not, therefore, be thought of as an attempt to give a definition of relevance. *See also* LOGIC, NORMAL-MODAL; LOGIC, PARACONSISTENT; LOGIC, SUBSTRUCTURAL; PARADOX; PROPOSITIONAL VARIABLE. [MJ]

Logic, Substructural. A logic is substructural if it does not validate all the structural rules and axioms of classical logic.

Rules and axioms of logics can be divided roughly into two different types. There are those that introduce and eliminate connectives (e.g. the axiom $A \to (B \to (A \land B))$) which can be used to introduce conjunctions) and those which manipulate the formulae and arguments in other ways. The latter type of axioms and rules are called structural axioms and rules.

The axiom $(A \to (B \to C)) \to (B \to (A \to C))$ does not introduce or remove connectives, rather it informs us that the order in which antecedents appear is not important. The axiom performs a similar role to the structural rule exchange (or permutation): if $\Delta, A, B \therefore C$ is a valid argument then so is $\Delta, B, A \therefore C$. This rule ensures that the order of premises does not matter for validity. (Note: for exchange to be worth considering Δ, A, B cannot be a set of assumptions, in this entry collections of assumptions will be assumed to be sequences rather than sets.)

Viewing logics as combining core rules for connectives and additional structural rules is a powerful approach to a wide range of logics.

The formula $p \to (q \to p)$ is not a theorem of any relevant logic. With the standard rule for introducing $\to$ and the structural rule weakening (also called thinning: if $\Delta \therefore C$ is valid then so is $\Delta, A \therefore C$) the formula $p \to (q \to p)$

can be proved. Relevant logics, thus, reject the weakening rule making them substructural logics.

The substructural logic BCK (as well as some relevant logics and linear logic) rejects the rule of contraction (if Δ, A, A ∴ C is valid, then so is Δ, A ∴ C).

Lambek calculus is used in mathematical linguistics and category theory. The premisses of an argument are thought of as grammatical phrases of a language. Placing a noun phrase after a verb phrase is not the same as placing a verb phrase before a noun phrase – thus, the rule exchange (as well as weakening and contraction) is dropped in Lambek calculus. *See also* ARGUMENT; ASSUMPTION; AXIOM; CONNECTIVES; LOGIC, RELEVANT; LOGIC, LINEAR; PREMISS; VALIDITY. [CA]

Logic, Temporal. Temporal logic aims to formalize temporal discourse and to model various conceptions of the nature of time (e.g. as linear, as branching, as having a beginning, as having no beginning).

Susan Haack (1978. *Philosophy of Logics*. Cambridge: Cambridge University Press, 156–62) distinguishes between two main approaches to temporal logic. On one, adopted by A.N. Prior (1957. *Time and Modality*. Oxford: Oxford University Press), tensed language is considered primitive. Temporal operators are employed, the syntactic functioning of which is analogous to that of the necessity and possibility operators of modal logic. Common temporal operators, with their interpretations, are: '**F**' ('It will be the case that . . . '), '**P**' ('It was the case that . . . '), '**G**' ('It will always be the case that . . . '), '**H**' ('It has always been the case that . . . '). As an example of a temporal sentence, take 'Mary visited Santiago'. Assign the sentence 'Mary is visiting Santiago' to the propositional variable 'A'. We can then translate 'Mary visited Santiago' as: PA ('It was the case that Mary is visiting Santiago'). For introductory material on this approach, see James W. Garson, (2006. *Modal Logic for Philosophers*. Cambridge: Cambridge University Press, 1, 50–2, 99–104).

On the other approach, associated with W.V.O. Quine, tensed language is considered dispensable. Temporality is dealt with by quantifying over times and using the primitive predicate '<' (interpreted as ' . . . is earlier than . . . '). The approach is based on predicate logic, not modal logic. Where 't' is a variable ranging over times, we can translate 'Mary visited Santiago' as: $(\exists t)[(t < now) \wedge Vms(t)]$ ('There is a time, t, earlier than now and Mary is visiting Santiago at *t'*). *See also* LOGIC; LOGIC, NORMAL-MODAL; LOGIC, PREDICATE; LOGICAL OPERATOR; NECESSITY; QUANTIFICATION; VARIABLE; PRIOR, ARTHUR NORMAN; QUINE, WILLARD VAN ORMAN. [SML]

Logical Consequence. A sentence *A* is a logical consequence of a set of premisses Γ if, whenever the premisses are true, the conclusion *A* is true. Consider the following example of a logically valid argument:

All men are mortal.
Socrates is a man.
Therefore Socrates is mortal.

That the conclusion is a logical consequence of the premisses can be understood as follows: whenever we substitute non-logical terms of our language (e.g. 'men', 'man') for non-logical terms of the appropriate grammatical category (e.g. 'goats', 'goat') in the argument, if the resulting premisses are true, the resulting conclusion will also be. The intuition is that a logically valid argument is one which is valid or truth preserving only in virtue of the logical form of its constituents, that is, in our example, in virtue of being of the form:

All *X* are *Y*
a is *X*
Therefore *a* is *Y*

But logical consequence defined substitutionally as above would depend on what non-logical terms are actually available for substitution in our language. We can improve on this by moving to the following definition: *A* is a logical consequence of the set of sentences Γ if, however we interpret the non-logical terms occurring in *A* and Γ if the sentences in Γ are true under this interpretation, then so is *A*. We say that we have interpreted a non-logical term when we have assigned an appropriate extension to it, be there or not a non-logical term actually having this semantic value in our language.

A last generalization yields the standard model-theoretic account of logical consequence: *A* is a logical consequence of Γ if and only if every model of Γ is a model of *A*. Since a model is defined as a nonempty set (domain) together with an interpretation of the non-logical terms over that domain, when checking if *A* logically follows from Γ we now must verify that *A* is true when Γ is under all interpretations of their non-logical terms and for all non-empty domains. *See also* COMPLETENESS; INFERENCE; INFERENCE, RULES OF; MODEL; MODEL-THEORY. [HG]

Logical Equivalence. A relation between logical forms. Logically equivalent forms are in some sense the same. They are in that their truth-values are the same in every interpretation; thus they represent different ways of expressing a particular truth-function. Since we cannot make one form true and the other false simultaneously, logically equivalent forms are said to imply each other.

'$\neg A_1 \vee \neg A_2$' is logically equivalent to '$\neg(A_1 \wedge A_2)$' but not to '$A_1 \vee A_2$'. If one form is equivalent to a second and that second to a third, then the first is equivalent to the third. *See also* IMPLICATION; INFERENCE; LOGICAL FORM; TRUTH-VALUE. [CF]

Logical Form. The logical form of a proposition is its internal structure. In particular, the logical form captures both the grammatical structure of a proposition and the logical relations among its components.

Consider the following sentence: If every French person is European, then every Parisian is European. If propositional calculus were to be used to formalize that sentence and we used the two propositional variables P and Q respectively to stand for the enclosed sentences within the main one, this would run as follows: if P, then Q. But in the main sentence there seems to be more than just that. As a matter of fact, the propositional calculus does not capture many features of natural language: it can only capture the logical relations between propositions as a whole, so that it fails to mirror their internal structure. Aristotelian analysis, though more elaborate than propositional calculus, can also translate a relatively narrow range of cases. The sentence above is easily translated into Aristotelian terms as: if every F is G, then every H is G. In order to see the limits of Aristotelian analysis, consider first the following example: '4 is bigger than 3'. As Aristotelian analysis exploits no relational predicates, the latter sentence is to be translated as follows: a is F. Second, Aristotelian analysis cannot account for quantification which is not in the subject position. Consider in fact the following example: some people love some pop singer. Aristotelian analysis forces us to treat 'love some pop singer' as a whole without recognizing the quantification within the predicate, so that the sentence should be translated as follows: some A is F, which is clearly not what the example says.

The flaw of Aristotelian logic is that it analyses propositions through the grammatical distinction between subject and predicate. Gottlob Frege came up with a different analysis, the logical analysis of argument-function, which accounts both for relational predication and quantification within grammatical predicates, and for the logical form of propositions. The system of logic he proposed in his *Begriffsschrift* is basically first-order predicate logic, where, besides the usual truth-functional connectives of propositional logic, there are individual variables $x, y, z, \ldots$ which vary over a domain of individuals, predicate constants $F, G, H, \ldots$ that stand for properties, and existential and universal quantification. *See also* ARGUMENT; LOGIC, PREDICATE; PROPOSITION; PROPOSITIONAL CALCULUS; QUANTIFICATION; SYLLOGISM; TRUTH-FUNCTIONAL; VARIABLE; FREGE, GOTTLOB; BEGRIFFSSCHRIFT. [FB]

Logical Function. A logical function is a relation that associates every element x of a set α to one, and only one, element y of a set β. The set α is said to be the domain of the function and β is said to be its range. *See also* DOMAIN; SET. [FB]

Logical Operator. An operation on one or more sentences. The truth-value of the resultant sentence depends on the truth-values of the sentences the logical operator is applied to. A unary logical operator takes a single sentence as its argument. An example is negation, which returns *true* when the argument is *false* and vice versa. A binary logical operator takes two sentences as its arguments. Examples are conjunction, disjunction and material implication. Two-valued logic has 4 unary logical operators and 16 binary ones. In digital electronic circuits, logical operators are implemented as logic gates. *See also* BINARY; CONJUNCTION; DISJUNCTION; MATERIAL IMPLICATION; NEGATION; SENTENCE; TRUTH-VALUE. [KV]

Logicism. Logicism is the philosophical view, advocated by Frege and supported among others by Russell and Carnap, that a substantial portion of mathematics, including at least arithmetic, is reducible to logic.

Logicism originated with Frege's criticism of the Kantian thesis that mathematics, including geometry and arithmetic, is constituted by synthetic a priori statements. Frege agreed with Kant on the synthetic nature of geometry, but considered arithmetic to be analytic and thus reducible to logic. Russell and Carnap, influenced by a more stringent criticism of Kantian synthetic a priori and by Hilbert's axiomatization of geometry, extended the programme of logicism to the whole of mathematics, including geometry.

In order to understand the difficulties faced by logicism, it is enough to consider the programme of reducing arithmetic to logic. Logicism had to perform two main tasks: (i) to define every arithmetic concept using only logical means; (ii) to show that every arithmetic true statement can be logically proved. An example of the first task is Russell's definition of natural number as the class of all classes that have the same number of elements; two classes have the same number of elements when there is a one-to-one correspondence between their elements. Such an approach relies on a naïve notion of class, which turned out to be afflicted by paradoxes. Russell devised type theory in order to overcome these paradoxes, but the logical validity of the axioms of type theory was far from evident. For example, there is no logical basis for the axiom of infinity, which affirms the existence of an infinite number of individuals: the universe could be finite with a finite number of objects.

The second task encountered even more difficulties. In order to show that every true arithmetic statement can be logically proved, logicism tried to reduce Peano arithmetic to logic. The main problem concerned the axiom of induction; it affirms that, given a generic property P, every natural number has the property P if the following two conditions hold:

(i) the number zero has the property P;
(ii) for every natural number n, if n has the property P then also $n+1$ has the property P.

It was hoped that a consistency proof for Peano arithmetic would show the logical validity of the axiom of induction. The fallacy of this line of thought emerged with Gödel's incompleteness theorems, which revealed that: (i) Peano arithmetic is incomplete (therefore there are true arithmetic statements that cannot be logically proved); (ii) a consistency proof for Peano arithmetic requires methods that are stronger than the axiom of induction itself (thus the logical validity of the axiom of induction cannot be based on a consistency proof for Peano arithmetic). *See also* ANALYTIC / SYNTHETIC; A PRIORI / A POSTERIORI; CONSISTENCY; MATHEMATICAL INDUCTION; PARADOX; TYPE THEORY; CARNAP, RUDOLF; FREGE, GOTTLOB; GÖDEL, KURT; HILBERT, DAVID; PEANO, GIUSEPPE; RUSSELL, BERTRAND. [MMu]

Löwenheim-Skolem. *See* THEOREMS.

Material Equivalence. Also known as 'biconditional', material equivalence (symbols: $a \leftrightarrow b$) is a 2-ary sentential operator that holds if and only if its operands a and b have the same truth-value: if a is true then b is true; if a is false then b is false. The biconditionality of material equivalence means that it proceeds as a twofold conditional, namely: $(a \leftrightarrow b) = [(a \to b) \land (b \to a)]$.

A distinction is to be made between material and formal (or logical) equivalence: the latter means that the corresponding material equivalence is logically true, that is, true under every interpretation of its components. *See also* BICONDITIONAL. [FS]

Mathematical Induction. A proof method that is typically used to prove a given statement for all natural numbers. The resulting proof is equivalent to an infinite number of proofs, each proving the statement for another natural number. A proof by mathematical induction is done in two steps: the base case and the inductive step. In the base case, one proves that the statement holds for the first natural number $n=0$. In the inductive step one proves that if the statement holds for a natural number $n=m$, then it also holds for the next one, $n=m+1$. The assumption in the inductive step that the statement holds for $n=m$ is called the induction hypothesis. In the inductive step, one uses this assumption to prove the statement for $n=m+1$. Mathematical induction works because if one can prove a statement for $n=0$ and one can prove that the statement holds for a value m, it still holds for $m+1$, then this process can go on indefinitely, that is, for all natural numbers. There exist variants of mathematical induction, the simplest of which starts with another value than 0 in the base case. *See also* ASSUMPTION; HYPOTHESIS; PROOF. [KV]

Meaning. A linguistic expression says something about the world by virtue of its meaning. The systematic study of meaning is the object of semantics.

Starting at least from the Stoics, logicians distinguish two different semantic notions, respectively called, in modern terminology, 'extension' and 'intension'. Given an expression E of a language L, its *extension* is the thing designated by E, whereas its *intension* is the way in which E designates that thing. For instance, the expressions 'Thales' and 'the first philosopher' have different intensions but the same extension, that is, Thales of Miletus. The intension–extension distinction is also known as the 'sense–reference', 'connotation–denotation' and *Sinn–Bedeutung* distinction (the last two German terms are due to Frege). Traditionally, the terms 'property' (or 'concept') and 'proposition' designate, respectively, the intension of a predicate (like 'philosopher') and of a declarative sentence (like 'Thales is a philosopher').

Building on Tarski's model-theoretic definition of truth, the semantical approach developed by Carnap, Hintikka and Montague defines the extension and the intension of E as follows. If E is a name (or a definite description), its extension is an individual; if E is a predicate, its extension is a class of individuals; if E is a sentence, its extension is a truth-value ('true' or 'false'). The intension of E is identified with the function that assigns to each possible world the extension of E in that world. Thus, for instance, the concept of philosopher (the intension of the predicate 'philosopher') is construed as the function that picks out from each possible world the extension of 'philosopher' – that is, the class of philosophers – in that world. E is a 'rigid designator' if, like proper names but contrary to definite descriptions, it has the same extension in every possible world. *See also* DEFINITE DESCRIPTION; INTENSION; MODEL THEORY; POSSIBLE WORLD; PROPERTY; PROPOSITION; SEMANTICS; TRUTH; FREGE, GOTTLOB. [GC]

Metalanguage. A metalanguage is a language which expresses the properties of another language, namely the object language. An example of an object language is the language of first order predicate logic. This latter language ascribes properties to individuals, but it can't ascribe properties to itself. In order to do that, we have to shift to the metalanguage of first-order predicate logic. For instance, the first-order proposition Fa may be true, but we can't assert this fact within first-order logic: in order to express the proposition '"Fa" is true' we have to resort to first-order logic's metalanguage. The requirement of the sharp distinction between a language and its metalanguage was first pointed out by Alfred Tarski in 1936: he showed that a first-order predicate logic can't express its own truth predicate, on pain of contradiction. It has to be stressed that for every formal language there is a corresponding metalanguage. There are infinitely many formal languages, for example, those of propositional logic, first-order predicate logic, second-order predicate logic and so forth, arranged in a hierarchy of languages distinct from one another according to the order of their predicates, from the most basic, namely propositional logic, to higher order predicate logics. These languages are of type 0, their respective metalanguages are of type 1, these latter's metalanguages are of type 2, and so on for every number n, so that there is also an infinite hierarchy of metalanguages for every order. Just as for every language of order *n*, there is a metalanguage, for every language of type *n*, there is a metalanguage of type *n*+1. *See also* CONTRADICTION; LOGIC, PREDICATE; LOGIC, PROPOSITIONAL; TARSKI, ALFRED. [FB]

Model. *See* INTERPRETATION.

Model Theory. All communication involves the production and interpretation of statements. Semantics studies the interpretations of statements. The study of the statements of a formal system is called metatheory. Metatheory may be divided into proof theory and model theory. Proof theory studies the rules guiding inferences within the system. Model theory is a mathematical approach to semantics, in particular to the assignment of truth-values to the statements of a theory.

A formal system consists of a language (vocabulary and formation rules) as well as axioms and rules for generating theorems. Given a formal system, the first step in model theory is to specify an interpretation of each symbol of the system. Then we provide rules governing the assignments of truth-values to complex expressions on the basis of assignments of truth-values to their component parts. A model is an interpretation of a system on which its theorems are true.

The semantics for the propositional calculus are easily given without model theory. Truth-tables suffice to interpret the connectives, and propositional variables can be replaced by propositions or sentences.

The semantics for predicate logic normally proceeds using set theory. We specify a domain of interpretation for the variables of the system. For example, it is natural to use the domain of natural numbers to model the Peano Axioms, and to use sets to model the axioms of set theory. Models of physical theories naturally take the physical world as their domains. Non-standard models, using unintended domains of quantification, are available.

The next step in constructing a model is to assign elements of the domain to symbols of the system. We assign particular objects to the constants. Predicates are normally interpreted as sets of objects in the domain, and n-place relations are taken as sets of ordered n-tuples within the domain. An existentially quantified sentence is true in a model if there is an object in the domain of interpretation with the properties mentioned in the sentence.

A universally quantified expression is true if the properties mentioned hold of every object in the domain.

For modal logics, Kripke models provide possible-worlds semantics. In a Kripke model, we start with a set of ordinary models, one for each possible world, and an accessibility relation among them. A statement is taken to be possible if there is an accessible possible world in which the statement is true. A statement is taken to be necessary if it is true in all possible worlds.

Model theory, developed in large part by Alfred Tarski and Abraham Robinson in the mid-twentieth century, has become a standard tool for studying set theory and algebraic structures. Major results of model theory include Paul Cohen's proof that the continuum hypothesis is independent of the axioms of Zermelo-Fraenkel (ZF) set theory including the axiom of choice, and that the axiom of choice itself is independent of the other axioms of ZF. Model theory is responsible for the so-called Skolem paradox, one of its earliest results. *See also* COMPLETENESS; FORMAL SYSTEM; INTERPRETATION; METALANGUAGE; MODEL; POSSIBLE WORLD; PROOF THEORY; PROPOSITIONAL CALCULUS; SET THEORY; SOUNDNESS; TRUTH-VALUE; HILBERT, DAVID; PEANO, GIUSEPPE; SKOLEN, THORALF; TARSKI, ALFRED. [RM]

Modus Ponens. *See* INFERENCE, RULES OF.

Modus Tollens. *See* INFERENCE, RULES OF.

Necessity. Necessity is usually said to apply to statements or propositions. A necessary proposition cannot fail to be true, has to be true, or, in the language of possible worlds, is true at/in all possible worlds. Possibility is the dual of necessity: to be possible is to be true at some possible world.

Although necessity and the a priori have been traditionally conceived as being intimately related, the prevalent, modern, Kripkean understanding of necessity strongly insists on the distinction between the two: necessity involves ontological or metaphysical matters only, whereas the a priori involves strictly epistemological ones: something is a priori if and only if it can be known independently of experience. Hence, in this modern reading, necessity and the a priori do not always coincide, something may be necessary without being a priori, and vice versa. Identity statements are typical examples of the necessary a posteriori: water is H_2O, necessarily, but this is only known a posteriori.

Examples of a priori statements that are not necessary (contingent a priori) are harder to come by and, as a general rule, more controversial. Most exploit rigid designators, such as Kripke's example of 'The standard meter measures one meter.' The proper name 'standard meter' denotes the same platinum rod in every possible world even though the accidental features of this rod may vary from one world to another. Therefore the standard meter does not necessarily measure one meter. However, it is argued that knowledge of the fact that the standard meter measures one meter is a priori.

Modal logic was initially developed to formally characterize necessity. As such, the axioms of modal logic have a natural 'necessity' reading, for example axiom T is usually interpreted as meaning that the actual world is possible. The predominant modal logic for necessity is S5. *See also* ANALYTIC / SYNTHETIC; A PRIORI / A POSTERIORI; LOGIC, NORMAL-MODAL; POSSIBLE WORLD; RIGID DESIGNATOR. [NK]

Negation. Negation is a truth-functional operator. It is expressed by each of the symbols '−', '~' or '¬', followed by a symbol, or a set of symbols, for a proposition, for example, ¬ p or ¬ ($p \lor q$). It denies the truth-value of the proposition it is applied to: if p is true, then ¬p is false, and vice versa. Two rules of natural deduction are associated with negation. The rule of *reductio ad absurdum* allows one to assume ¬p, when p has to be proved. If from ¬p a contradiction is derived, by *reductio* then p is indeed proved. The rule of double negation allows one to derive p from $\neg\neg p$. *See also* DOUBLE NEGATION; PROPOSITION; TRUTH-FUNCTIONAL; TRUTH-VALUE. [FB]

Negation as Failure. In logic programming, a negation operator is often implemented as 'negation as failure': if the program fails to derive A, then $\neg A$ is derived instead. In other words, falsity is identified with non-provability. Underlying this idea is the closed world assumption: the programme assumes that it knows all that there is to know; thus, what is not known to be true is false. The corresponding inference rule – from $\not\vdash A$ derive $\neg A$ – is non-classical, since its premise is not a formula of the language, but a meta-theoretic statement. This inference rule is nonmonotonic: that is, the addition of new premises may lead one to retract old conclusions. *See also* CLOSED WORLD ASSUMPTION; INFERENCE, RULE OF; LOGIC PROGRAMMING; RESOLUTION; LOGIC, NONMONOTONIC; NEGATION. [GC]

Nonmonotonic. *See* LOGIC, NONMONOTONIC.

Normal Form. A normal form of a mathematical object is a standard representation of this object. Every object has exactly one normal form and two objects with the same normal form are equivalent. For example, the logical formula $(\neg A \lor C) \land (A \lor B) \land (B \lor C)$ is equivalent to its disjunctive normal form $(\neg A \land B) \lor (A \land C)$. *See also* DISJUNCTIVE NORMAL FORM. [KV]

NP Complete. *See* COMPLEXITY.

Ontology (Domain). A representation of the things that exist within a particular domain of reality such as medicine, geography, ecology or law, as opposed to philosophical ontology, which has all of reality as its subject matter. A domain ontology provides a controlled, structured vocabulary to annotate data in order to make it more easily searchable by human beings and processable by computers. The Gene Ontology Project is an example of a domain ontology that attempts to provide a taxonomy and controlled vocabulary for genes and gene products. Domain ontologies benefit from research in formal ontology, which assists in making possible communication between and among ontologies by providing a common language and common formal framework for reasoning. *See also* DOMAIN; ONTOLOGY (FORMAL); ONTOLOGY (PHILOSOPHICAL). [RA]

Ontology (Formal). A discipline which assists in making possible communication between and among domain ontologies by providing a common language and common formal framework for reasoning. This communication is accomplished by (at least) the adoption of a set of basic categories of objects, discerning what kinds of entities fall within each of these categories of objects, and determining what relationships hold within and among the different categories in the domain ontology. Formal ontology draws heavily from the logic and methodology of philosophical ontology. Through the work of thinkers such as Edmund Husserl, Roman Ingarden, Barry Smith and Patrick Hayes, formal ontology is increasingly being applied in bioinformatics, intelligence analysis, management science and in other scientific fields, where it serves as a basis for the improvement of classification, information organization and automatic reasoning. *See also* DOMAIN; CATEGORY; LOGIC; ONTOLOGY (DOMAIN); ONTOLOGY (PHILOSOPHICAL). [RA]

Ontology (Philosophical). A branch of Western philosophy having its origins in ancient Greece in the work of philosophers such as Parmenides, Heraclitus, Plato and Aristotle. Philosophical ontology is concerned with the study of what is, of the kinds and structures of objects, properties, events, processes and relations in every area of reality.

The term 'ontology' derives from the Greek 'ontos' ('being' or 'what exists') and 'logos' ('rational account' or 'knowledge'). From the philosophical perspective, 'ontology' is synonymous with 'metaphysics' as classically conceived. This philosophical sense of the term is what Jacob Lorhard had in mind when he coined the term 'ontology' (*ontologia*) around 1613, and this is also why Bailey's 1721 Oxford English Dictionary defined ontology as 'an Account of being in the Abstract'. *See also* CATEGORIES; ONTOLOGY (DOMAIN); ONTOLOGY (FORMAL); ARISTOTLE. [RA]

Paradox. A paradox is a piece of reasoning that leads from apparently true premisses, via apparently acceptable steps of inference, to a conclusion that is contradictory or in some other way unacceptable. Typically, the reasoning is utterly simple, so it is very alarming that we should be led astray in this way, and we have to confront the real possibility that some of our deepest beliefs or most fundamental principles of inference are wrong. This is the reason why the study of paradoxes is so important. A satisfactory solution will not only expose the basic error afflicting a given paradox, but will also account for how we were taken in by it.

Here is W.V. Quine's lovely formulation of *The Barber of Alcala* paradox:

> Logicians tell of a village barber who shaves all those villagers – and only those – who do not shave themselves. The question of the barber's own toilet holds a certain fascination for the logical mind. For it has been agreed that the barber shaves any villager, *x*, if and only if *x* does not shave himself; hence when we let *x* be the barber, we conclude that he shaves himself if and only if he does not.

The assumptions here are: There is a village where shaving is *de rigueur* for adult males. Some shave themselves; all those who don't shave themselves get shaved by the sole barber in the village, himself an adult male needing to be shaved. Yet the assumption that he shaves himself leads to the conclusion that he does not (for his job is to shave only those who do not shave themselves); and the assumption that he does not shave himself leads to the conclusion that he does shave himself (because it's his job to shave precisely those who do not shave themselves).

Some philosophers hold that there is an easy solution to this paradox, namely to reject the assumption that there can be a village containing one adult male barber who shaves all and only those adult male villagers who do not shave themselves. Well, perhaps, but *Russell's paradox* has a structure similar to *The Barber*, yet no such easy solution seems available for it. The class of horses contains only horses as its members; in particular, it does not contain classes and so does not contain the class of horses. So the class of horses does not contain itself as a member; it is a non-self-membered class. By contrast, the class of all things that are not horses does contain itself as a member. Now consider the Russell Class *R* that contains all and only the non-self-membered classes. Does it contain itself as a member? The situation (compare the last sentence of Quine's formulation of *The Barber*) is that *R* contains any class *x* as a member if and only if *x* does not contain itself; hence when we let *x* be the Russell Class *R*, we conclude that *R* is a member of *R* if and only if it isn't! Can we now suggest, in parallel with what was suggested as a solution to *The Barber*, that *R* does not exist? Well, the class of horses exists, as do many other non-self-membered classes. And *R* just collects up all these non-self-membered classes. So how could it *not* exist?

Perhaps the most famous paradox, the discovery of which is attributed to the ancient Greek Eubulides, is called *The Liar* and concerns a person who says 'This statement is false.' You can quickly see that if the statement is true, then it is false and if false, is true. Let us make the assumption, then, that it is neither true nor false, that is, not true and *not false*. But then, since the statement claims itself to be false, it must be false – contrary to our assumption. One way out of this impasse is the Dialetheist proposal that the Liar statement, and others like it, are at once *both* true and false. A somewhat less outrageous solution (though it needs a lot of careful defending) is that the Liar *sentence* fails to make a *statement* and so does not get into the true/false game. A near-relation of the Liar is the *Curry-Löb Paradox*, one version of which takes as its starting point the statement 'If this statement is true, then pigs can fly.' Or consider this closely related version: 'Either this statement is false or pigs can fly.' That statement cannot be false, for if it were then the first disjunct would be true, hence the whole statement would be true. So it must be true, therefore the first disjunct is false, so the whole statement can be true only if the second judgement is true. Hence pigs can fly!

Of the ancient paradoxes attributed to Zeno of Elea, the most compelling concerns a race between swift *Achilles* and a tortoise who starts half way up the racetrack. The race begins, and Achilles quickly reaches the point where the tortoise was – but, of course, the tortoise has then moved a little bit ahead to a new point. When Achilles reaches that new point, the tortoise has moved ahead, if only a small distance. And so on. The argument seems to show that Achilles can never catch the tortoise, for whenever he reaches where the tortoise was, the tortoise is ahead. Yet commonsense, elementary mathematics, or watching a re-creation of the event discloses that Achilles *does* catch and overtake the tortoise.

The *Sorites Paradox*, in its original form, concerns a large number of grains of sand piled together, indisputably a heap. Surreptitiously remove one grain and you still have a heap, in fact the removal of one grain makes no perceptible difference. Remove another grain. Indistinguishable difference; still a heap . . . At no point will the removal of one grain transform a heap into a non-heap. But that seems to show that, continuing to remove one grain at a time, you will have to call a heap three grains of sand . . . two . . . one . . . nought! *See also* ASSUMPTION; CLASS; CONCLUSION; INFERENCE; PREMISS; INFERENCE; QUINE, WILLARD VAN ORMAN; RUSSELL, BERTRAND. [LG]

Possible World. Possible worlds are used to express modal statements involving possibility. In possible world talk, the statement 'Al Gore could have been president' is understood as saying that there exists a possible world *w* at/in which Al Gore is president. The modal 'could' is replaced by the indicative 'is' by use of quantification over possible worlds. Analogously, a statement such as 'Al Gore is necessarily human' is translated as: at every possible world, Al Gore is human. In general, the truth of a modal statement is thereby translated into a quantificational claim on worlds at which the indicative counterpart of this statement has a normal, indicative truth-value.

The need for such an account came from certain anomalies encountered with modalities: arguments previously thought to preserve truth no longer did with modal statements. For example, from the truth of the statements 'The number of planets = 8' and 'Necessarily, 8 = 8', we cannot conclude, substituting equals for equals, that 'Necessarily, the number of planets = 8' is true. With possible worlds, we easily understand why the conclusion fails, for simple quantificational reasons: the number of planets is 8 in some worlds, namely the actual, but not in all of them.

It must be noted that, however useful possible worlds are, their ontological status is a much debated philosophical issue. Some – modal realists – consider possible worlds as existent, concrete non-actual objects, others take them to be abstract, conceptual or representational only.

Possible worlds can also be understood in a broader, less metaphysical sense. Just as we understood possibility and necessity using possible worlds, we can understand epistemic and deontic modalities using epistemically and deontically 'possible' worlds respectively. Statement ϕ is conceivable (resp. a priori) iff ϕ is true at some (resp. all) epistemically possible worlds. *Mutatis mutandis* for ϕ is permissible (resp. obligatory). *See also* LOGIC, DEONTIC; LOGIC, EPISTEMIC; NECESSITY; QUANTIFICATION. [NK]

Postulate. 'Postulate' is frequently synonymous with 'axiom'. Postulates can be distinguished from axioms based on epistemic status or content. When distinguished epistemically, a postulate is a supposition; it might not be believed before being used in a demonstration. Alternatively, postulates have substantive content whereas axioms have only logical content. *See also* AXIOM. [AH]

Practical Syllogism. The practical syllogism is an analysis of deliberation, that is, reasoning aimed at action rather than belief. It originates with Aristotle, specifically in his *Nicomachean Ethics* and *On the Movement of Animals*. For Aristotle, a practical syllogism comprises a universal major premiss, which makes a general judgment as to the value of an activity, a particular minor premiss, which makes a specific claim of fact, and a conclusion, which is the action to be undertaken (or, on some interpretations, the decision so to act). For example, 'one conceives that every man ought to walk, one is a man oneself: straightaway one walks' (*Movement*, 701a12). Aristotle uses this account to explain the limitations of practical reasoning: when confronted by two opposing value judgments, each of which could comprise the major premiss of practical syllogisms resulting in incompatible courses of action, we choose that conclusion most in accordance with our desires.

Practical reasoning remains a pivotal topic in several disciplines. It is crucial to ethics, since it is concerned with the process of ethical decision-making, but it is also important to the philosophy of mind and debates over free will, as a component in the understanding of action. Moreover, the replication of practical reasoning is an important goal for artificial intelligence, and, as an instance of informal, defeasible reasoning, its systematization is within the scope of argumentation theory. In recent decades a great diversity of accounts of practical reasoning have been proposed. Instrumentalism, for which practical reasoning is limited to how we realize our desires, not which desires to realize, remains influential. Alternatives range from outright denial that practical reasoning is possible, to sophisticated choice procedures, such as the maximization of utility or the pursuit of coherence. *See also* ARGUMENTATION, THEORY OF; SYLLOGISM; ARISTOTLE. [AA]

Predicate. A predicate is a linguistic item that is used to assert that a property or relation holds. In predicate logic, predicates are expressed via uppercase letters A, B, . . . : '$P(c)$', for instance, means that c has property P. See also LOGIC, PREDICATE; PROPERTY. [MMo]

Predicate Logic. See LOGIC, PREDICATE.

Premiss. Every argument contains one or more premisses. Together, an argument's premisses are the starting assumptions from which a conclusion is to be derived. To be a premiss is to play a role in an argument; the same proposition may be a premiss of one argument but the conclusion of another. See also ARGUMENT; CONCLUSION; DEDUCTION; INDUCTION. [APM]

Probability. A mathematical theory with many important applications in science and philosophy. Its historical origins lie in a correspondence between Fermat and Pascal; it was further developed by (among others) Bernoulli and Laplace, and received its canonical formulation in Kolmogorov's *Foundations of the Theory of Probability* of 1933. Since then, other versions of the theory have been presented, but Kolmogorov's treatment remains the most widely accepted one.

Kolmogorov defines the probability function p in the following way. For some non-empty set Ω and the set Φ of all subsets of Ω that are closed under union and complementation, p is a mapping between the elements of Φ and the real numbers that satisfies the following three axioms: (1) For any subset A of Φ: $p(A) \geq 0$; (2) $p(\Omega) = 1$; (3) For all non-overlapping subsets A, B of Φ: $p(A \cup B) = p(A) + p(B)$. To this Kolmogorov adds the following definition of a conditional probability (though it may be worthwhile to consider this simply as a fourth axiom): for all subsets A, B of Φ: $p(A|B) = p(A \cap B) / p(B)$, if $p(B) \neq 0$. Finally, Kolmogorov controversially suggests adding an axiom of continuity to (1)–(3) that entails that (3) also holds for countably many subsets of Φ.

Intuitively, these axioms make clear that, on the one hand, all assignments of probabilities must be between 0 and 1, with the certain event – that is, the union of all possible events – having probability 1. On the other, they state that the probability of one of two mutually exclusive events happening is the sum of their individual probabilities, and that the probability of an event A conditional on another event B is the probability they happen jointly, normalized by the probability that B happens.

Given an initial assignment of probability values, these axioms make it possible to determine some or all of the other values of a probability function. So, for example, the axioms ensure that, if we know that $p(A) = 1/2$ and $p(B|A) = p(B|\neg A) = 2/5$, we can compute that $p(B) = 2/5$ (this follows from the definition of conditional probability and axiom [3]). The axioms also allow one to prove several well-known theorems: for example, they make it easy to show that $p(A|B) = p(B|A) \, p(A) \, / \, p(B)$ (Bayes' Theorem) and that $p(A) = p(A|B) \, p(B) + p(A|\neg B) \, p(\neg B)$ (the 'law of total probability').

These and similar results have turned out to be very useful in many branches of science and philosophy. In particular, probability theory has come to form the core of statistics (the analysis of quantitative data), is a major element of quantum mechanics and the theory of evolution (the major theories at the heart of much of modern physics and modern biology, respectively) and has been used as an extension of traditional logic. In this manner, the introduction of probabilities into science has led to many major advances in our understanding of how the world works and has significantly broadened our mathematical toolkit in the process. *See also* AXIOM; BAYES' THEOREM; LOGIC, PROBABILISTIC; PROBABILITY, INTERPRETATION OF; SET; THEORY. [AWS]

Probability, Interpretation of. An interpretation of probability is a theory of the meaning of expressions involving the formal notion of probability. Mathematically, a probability is just a specific kind of function that is fully defined by its axioms and definitions. However, various thinkers thought it valuable to go beyond this technical view of probabilities and to attach a 'deeper' meaning to them. Alas, it has turned out to be very controversial what, exactly, that meaning is – in particular, there are no less than four major interpretations of probability currently being defended.

First, the Frequency Interpretation says that probabilities are statements about the limits of infinite sequences. For example, saying that the probability of this coin landing heads is 0.5 is taken to express the claim that in an infinitely long sequence of tosses, the ratio of heads to tails will be 1:1. According to this interpretation, then, probabilities are only defined relative to some 'reference class' (in this case, the set of tosses), and, being limits, are not directly measurable.

It is in particular this last fact that has led to inception of the second interpretation: the Propensity Theory. On this view, a probability expresses the tendency of some particular process to have some particular outcome. For example, saying that the probability of this coin landing hands is 0.5 is taken to express the proposition that the coin has the tendency to land hands about 50% of the time when tossed. A major (if controversial) benefit of this interpretation is that it makes probabilities easily measurable; a major (but also controversial) disadvantage is that its core concept – that of a 'propensity' – is quite mysterious.

The third view – the Logical Interpretation – takes probabilities to express degrees of entailment among propositions. On this view, a 0.5 probability of this coin landing heads is taken to mean that the proposition 'this coin is being tossed' entails the proposition 'this coin lands heads' to degree 0.5. This interpretation thus generalizes the classical notion of entailment; however, it faces the problem that no fully compelling method for specifying the degree of entailment among two propositions has yet been found.

The final interpretation, the Subjective Theory, sees probabilities as expressions of subjectively rational degrees of belief. Saying that there is a 0.5 probability that this coin will land heads is taken to express a particular agent's rational degree of belief in the coin landing heads. The main advantage of this interpretation is that it permits probabilities to be applied in many areas of the social sciences (where beliefs play a crucial role); the trouble is that it does not allow for a unique probability assignment to the occurrence of an event.

It is important to note that, while each of these interpretations still has some defenders, not everybody thinks that a commitment to any one of them is necessary. Instead, some people advertise a pluralist position (according to which different interpretations are acceptable in different circumstances) and some see probabilities as theoretical terms that are not in need of explicit interpretation at all. *See also* BAYESIANISM; FUNCTION; INTERPRETATION; LOGIC, PROBABILISTIC; PROBABILITY; PROPOSITION; CARNAP, RUDOLF. [AWS]

Proof. There are at least two senses of 'proof' relevant to logic: formal proof and informal proof. Each provides a kind of justification for some claim.

A formal proof comes within a specified formal system: a language, perhaps some axioms (for which no proofs are given), and rules. The goal is to arrive at the claim (formula) on the last line of the proof. Each line must be either an axiom (if any) or obtained from previous lines by an application of a rule. Typically, a proof will begin with assumed premises of an argument. The trick is to apply rules in order to have the conclusion on the last line. Once this is done, it has been demonstrated that the conclusion does follow from the premises. Unless we challenge the rules, there can be no questioning this.

An informal proof is modelled on formal proofs. However, in an informal proof, the demonstration is conducted externally to any formal system that might be under discussion. Nonetheless, certain starting points are assumed, and the goal is to reason in secure steps from these to the claim being established. These steps are not mechanically verifiable as they are in a formal proof. *See also* ARGUMENT; DEDUCTION; FORMAL SYSTEM. [CF]

Proof Theory. Proof theory is a branch of logic that began with work by David Hilbert and that has as central the notion of proof in a formal system.

The notion of formal system is the result of a process of formalization of axiomatic theories. Generally speaking, a formal system is based on a language in which we fix the primitive symbols and the rules that determine its terms and its formulae, and consists of a decidable set of axioms and a decidable set of rules of inference (a set S is said to be decidable if, and only if, there exists an uniform procedure by means of which it is possible to establish, in a finite number of steps, if, for each object x, x belongs to S or not). A proof in a formal system is simply a finite sequence of formulae, each of which is either an axiom, or is derived by one of the inference rules from the preceding formulae. The last formula of a proof is said to be a theorem.

Hilbert's programme consisted in the attempt to: (1) formalize mathematical theories, that is, reduce mathematics to formal systems, (2) prove, by means of finitary methods (that is to say methods that use only finite or verifiable means), their consistency, that is, prove that formal systems do not imply any contradiction. This way Hilbert believed that mathematics could be justified. Note that once intuitive mathematical theories have been substituted by corresponding formal systems, they become rigorously defined objects in their own right, meriting the same sort of treatment as other, more traditional and familiar, mathematical objects. Their study usually takes the name of 'meta-mathematics'; the proof of the consistency of a formal system, for example, is a meta-mathematical result.

Hilbert's programme was brought to a halt by Gödel's results, according to which it is impossible to prove by means of finitary methods the consistency of the elementary theory of numbers.

It was Hilbert's student Gerhard Gentzen who picked up the themes of Hilbertian proof theory, and put them through a new analysis, in order to revive them despite Gödel's negative results. Gentzen created a new type of formal system, namely natural deduction systems, in which we can construct mathematical proofs that are closer simulations of our actual way of reasoning in mathematics. Furthermore, by generalizing these systems, he obtained the calculi called the sequent calculi and proved some important results. One (the Hauptsatz) says that, for any provable formula, there exists a proof in which the only expressions that occur in it are subformulas of the formula that we want to prove; that is to say, for any provable formula, there exists an analytic proof of it. The second important result concerns the consistency of arithmetical formal systems that he managed to prove by using transfinite induction. This principle, though it was not finitary and therefore did not fit in with Hilbert's programme, nevertheless presents characteristics of high constructivity and it is intuitionistically acceptable.

These results are the basis of the important developments of the modern, post-Hilbertian proof theory, some of which constitute real and autonomous fields. [FP]. *See also* DECIDABILITY; THEORY; GÖDEL, KURT; HILBERT, DAVID; HILBERT'S PROGRAMME.

Property. A property is an attribute, feature or quality (e.g. the property 'red'). A property may be a defining characteristic of some class, entity, function or process: for example, the even numbers have the property that multiplication of even numbers results in an even number; this property may be thought of as one of the properties that characterizes the even numbers. *See also* ASSUMPTION; AXIOM; INTERPRETATION. [JG]

Proposition. A proposition asserts that a certain state of affairs obtains. 'It is raining (at a given place and time)', 'Snow is white', 'New York is the capital of Belgium', all express propositions. Propositions have truth-values, and in classical logic propositions are exclusively either true or false, depending on whether or not the state of affairs they affirm actually exists. The proposition that *snow is white* is true, whereas the proposition that *New York is the capital of Belgium* is false. Propositions are different from interrogatives that ask questions, and imperatives that issue commands or make requests, which do not have truth-values. Propositions are often described as the abstract meanings of concrete sentences, in somewhat the way that numbers are said to be the abstract referents of numerals. *See also* LOGIC; SENTENCE; STATEMENT, COMPOUND; STATEMENT, SIMPLE; TRUTH-VALUE. [DJ]

Proposition, Particular Affirmative (I). *See* SQUARE OF OPPOSITION.

Proposition, Particular Negative (O). *See* SQUARE OF OPPOSITION.

Proposition, Universal Affirmative (A). *See* SQUARE OF OPPOSITION.

Proposition, Universal Negative (E). *See* SQUARE OF OPPOSITION.

Propositional Calculus. *See* LOGIC, PROPOSITIONAL.

Propositional Function. Also known as 'sentential function' (Tarski) and 'open sentence' (especially in mathematical logic), this was Frege's technical term for a function (such as 'x is F') in which one or more places of a sentence are taken by variables. Such functions enable us to move from arguments to (truth-bearing) propositions once definite values have been assigned to all the variable components, turning the latter into constants (e.g. 'Smith is happy'). *See also* PROPOSITION; PROPOSITIONAL VARIABLE; FREGE, GOTTLOB. [CS]

Propositional Variable. A propositional variable is a variable interpreted as ranging over propositions. A propositional variable is assigned a truth-value, that is, the true or the false, depending on whether the proposition it stands for is true or false. *See also* PROPOSITION; TRUTH-VALUE; VARIABLE. [FB]

Quantification. In predicate logic quantification refers to the variable-binding application of one or more quantifiers (e.g. *some, all, every, any, most* etc.) to an open sentence. Thus, for example, the free variables of the function '*Fx*' ['*x* is *F*'] become bound by the existential quantifier ($\exists$) in the following way: ($\exists x$) *Fx* ['there exists some *x* that is *F*']. Similarly, the universal quantifier ($\forall$) operates on the previously free variables as follows: ($\forall x$) *Fx* ['all *x* are *F*']. Formal quantification thus captures certain relations more precisely than Aristotelian logic does, since Aristotelian logic takes individual and general predication to have the same logical form. The application of formal quantification to *natural language* is, however, philosophically contentious. For example, ($\forall$) is typically used to cover a range of quantifying terms (such as 'for every', 'for all', and 'for any') which pick out distinct concepts in ordinary language.

Since Frege, *singular* first-order existential and universal quantification have generally been held to be the two most *fundamental* types of quantification. Complex quantifiers thought to be expressible in terms of combinations of ($\exists$) and ($\forall$) include the uniqueness quantifier ('$\exists!$') ['there exists one *and only* one'] and the counting quantifier ($\exists k$) ['there exists a natural number *k*']. *See also* QUANTIFIER; ARISTOTLE; FREGE, GOTTLOB. [CS]

Quantification Rules. The Quantification Rules govern inferences on propositions where one of the two quantifiers is the main operator. There are four such rules: a generalization and instantiation rule for each of the two quantifiers. Universal Generalization (UG), Universal Instantiation (UI), Existential Generalization (EG) and Existential Instantiation (EI). Generalization rules allow one to add, while instantiation rules allow one to remove, a quantifier. Existential Generalization endorses the inference from 'Ursula runs' to 'Someone runs', which is rendered formally as the inference from R*u* to ($\exists x$)R*x*. Universal Instantiation endorses the inference from 'Everyone quits' to 'Victor quits'; formally rendered as the inference from ($\forall y$)Q*y* to Q*v*. Universal Generalization endorses the inference from T*w* to ($\forall x$)T*x*, but only where *w* names an arbitrary individual. Different systems guarantee arbitrariness differently, though usually by prohibiting the relevant name from appearing in the premises or conclusion of the argument. (EG and UI are not similarly restricted.) Existential Instantiation is challenging to apply correctly. Some systems allow the inference from ($\exists x$)S*x* to S*v*, so long as *v* names an arbitrary individual. Other systems disallow this direct inference, but allow the instance (*Sv* in our example) to serve as an assumption in a subderivation within the original proof. *See also* INFERENCE, RULES OF; LOGIC, PREDICATE; SQUARE OF OPPOSITION. [APM]

Quantifier. Quantifiers allow the formalization of claims regarding quantities ('Everyone thinks', 'Something smells'). The 'universal quantifier', $(\forall x)$, represents 'every' or 'all', while the 'existential quantifier', $(\exists x)$, represents 'some' or 'at least one'. An individual variable (x, y or z) must follow the quantifier symbol, but any variable can be used, for example, $(\forall y)$ and $(\exists z)$. *See also* LOGIC, PREDICATE; QUANTIFICATION; QUANTIFICATION RULES; SQUARE OF OPPOSITION. [APM]

Recursion. Recursion is a process whereby an object is defined in terms of previously defined objects similar to itself. For example, the natural numbers can be defined thus:

1 is a natural number (this is referred to as the *base case*);
if *n* is a natural number, then *n*+1 is also a natural number (*recursion step*).

To put it another way, given the definition of 1 as a natural number, it follows that each natural number has a successor, which is also a natural number.

Recursive definitions, particularly useful in logic and computer science, are the cornerstone of the theory of computation, as developed by Alan Turing and others in the 1930s. Of particular interest to philosophers are the recursive functions, which are central to Gödel's incompleteness theorems. *See also* THEOREMS; GÖDEL, KURT; TURING, ALAN. [DH]

Resolution. The Resolution Rule is a technique of automated theorem proving, based on the fact that all sentences in propositional logic have an equivalent in conjunctive normal form. This rule, which also works for predicate logic, is often used together with reductio ad absurdum and states that if we are given two clauses in conjunctive normal form, one containing *X* and the other containing not-*X*, then we can infer the union of those two clauses, without *X* and not-*X*. The seminal work in this area is by J. Alan Robinson (1965. A machine-oriented logic based on the resolution principle. *Journal of the ACM*, 12(1): 23–41), in which he lays the foundation for automated theorem proving. *See also* AXIOMATIZATION; LOGIC, PROPOSITIONAL; NORMAL FORM; REFUTATION. [DH]

Rigid Designator. *See* MEANING.

Russell's Programme. *See* LOGICISM.

Scope. The scope of something is what that thing applies to. We can make this more precise. The scope of a connective is the well-formed formula of which that connective is the main connective. The scope of another logical operator such as a quantifier or a modal operator is the first complete well-formed formula that follows that operator.

For example, consider (1): (∃x)(Qx∨ Rx) ∨ Sx. The scope of the existential quantifier is (Qx∨ Rx).

Now consider (2): ((A∨B)→C)∧D). The scope of the '→' does not include the conjunction operator. *See also* CONNECTIVES; LOGICAL OPERATOR; QUANTIFIER. [CF]

Semantic Tree. In propositional logic, we can determine whether a set of formulae is consistent by examining the truth-tables for the set. Alternatively, we can construct a semantic tree. Semantic trees may be used to test an argument for validity, since an argument is invalid if, and only if, the negation of its conclusion is consistent with the truth of its premisses. Semantic trees are less cumbersome than truth-tables, providing an easy method for testing a large set of formulae. They require less creative construction than natural deductions. There are decision procedures for semantic trees for propositional logic, which means that the procedure will always terminate in a solution.

To construct a semantic tree, we replace compound formulae with simpler sub-formulae with the same truth-conditions. For example, we can replace '¬(A ∨ B)' with '¬A' and '¬B', since the longer formula is true if, and only if, the shorter ones are true (see Figure 5). Some replacement rules branch, giving the construction the appearance of a tree. For example, any branch on which 'A → B' appears divides into two branches, one which contains '¬A' and the other which contains 'B' (see Figure 6). The tree is completely constructed when all compound formulae have been replaced by either simple formulae or negations of simple formulae. If all branches contain a contradiction (a simple propositional formula and its negation) then the original set of formulae is inconsistent.

Semantic trees are useful in predicate logic, as well. For sets of formulae with only monadic predicates, the rules determine a decision procedure. There is no decision procedure for some sets of formulae with relational predicates. Semantic trees are also useful in modal logic.

Semantic trees are also called truth-trees or semantic tableaux.

1. ¬(A ∨ B)

|

2. ¬A
3. ¬B

Figure 5 Semantic tree for ¬(A ∨ B).

1.   A → B

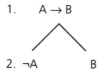

2. ¬A   B

Figure 6 Semantic tree for A→B.

See also CONSISTENCY; DEDUCTION; LOGIC, PREDICATE; PROOF; TRUTH-TABLE; VALIDITY. [RM]

Semantics. Logics may be defined syntactically by deductive calculi that include a formal language. Proof theory investigates a logic from the point of view of deducibility and provability, however, logics are often motivated by an intended interpretation of their symbols, and it is desirable to specify an interpretation formally. The interpretation of the logical symbols is the same in all interpretations, whereas the interpretation of the nonlogical symbols may vary to some extent. An interpretation of a logic is called a model for the logic. Semantics and model theory comprise the models of a logic and the investigation of their properties. For example, Boole gave two different interpretations of his algebra of logic.

The first rigorous definition of a semantics for classical first-order logic was given in the mid-1930s. Assuming that the language contains ¬ ('not'), ∨ ('or') and ∀ ('for all') as logical constants, denumerably many variables $x_0, x_1, x_2, \ldots$, and predicate symbols $P_1^{n1}, P_2^{n2}, \ldots$ as nonlogical symbols, the interpretation may be outlined as follows. Let D be a nonempty set of arbitrary objects (the domain), I an interpretation function and v a valuation function.

1. $I(\neg\varphi)_v = T$ iff $I(\varphi)_v = F$,
2. $I(\varphi_i \vee \varphi_j)_v = T$ iff $I(\varphi_i)_v = T$ or $I(\varphi_j)_v = T$,

3. $I\,(P_i^{ni}(x_1,\ \ldots,\ x_{ni}))_v = T$ iff $<v(x_1),\ \ldots,\ v(x_{ni})> \in I\,(P_i^{ni})$,
4. $I\,(\forall x.\ \varphi)_v = T$ iff for any valuation $v[x \mapsto d]$, $I\,(\varphi)_{v[x\,\alpha\,d]} = T$,

where $v[x \mapsto d]$ is a one-point modification of the valuation function setting x's value to d (where $d \in D$).

The relationship between a logic and its semantics is expressed by the soundness and the completeness theorems. An axiomatization of first-order classical logic is sound if φ's provability from Γ implies that every interpretation mapping all elements of Γ into T, interpret φ into T. Completeness states the converse, that is, if φ is a semantic consequence of the set of formulae Γ, then φ is derivable from Γ.

Nonclassical logics require more intricate interpretations than classical logic does. A semantics may include 3, 4, finitely many or infinitely many values. A logic may have algebraic semantics, where the logical constants are mapped into operations and constants of the algebra. A semantics – often used in completeness proofs – may be built from expressions (or equivalence classes of expressions) of the logic, some of which are called 'term semantics'.

The preferred type of semantics for nonclassical logics is the relational semantics. Kripke introduced such semantics for normal modal logics, and they are nowadays usually called 'possible worlds semantics'. In relational semantics, sentences are interpreted as propositions, which are sets of possible worlds or situations. Those connectives that do not occur in classical logic are defined from a compatibility (or accessibility) relation on situations. Relational semantics for relevance logics utilizing a ternary accessibility relation were introduced by Routley and Meyer. A uniform framework – called generalized Galois logics – encompassing relational semantics for nonclassical logics was introduced by Dunn. A precise characterization of classes of relational structures for a logic can be obtained by adding a topology to the structures. This leads straightforwardly to dualities between the categories of algebras of logics and of relational structures for logics. *See also* COMPLETENESS; DOMAIN; INTERPRETATION; MODEL THEORY; PREDICATE; POSSIBLE WORLD; PROOF THEORY; PROPOSITION; SOUNDNESS; THEOREMS; BOOLE, GEORGE; KRIPKE, SAUL. [KB]

Sentence. A sentence is a string of words that obey the rules of grammar of a given language. Its meaning is a proposition and its utterance by a speaker results in a statement. The interrelation between sentence, proposition and statement varies according to one's philosophical position about how the meaning of a sentence is established. *See also* PROPOSITION. [FS]

Set. A set is a collection of objects, called members or elements, that is itself an object. According to Cantor, a set is 'a multiplicity that is also a unity'. Sets are extensional: If the membership of a set is determined, then the identity of the set is determined. *See also* ABSTRACTION; CLASS; PARADOX; CANTOR, GEORG; FREGE, GOTTLOB. [ZW]

Set Theory. Set theory has two main aspects. The first is to serve the study of the mathematical infinite, describing various quantitative, combinatorial and ordering properties of sets of numbers and points. The second is to serve as a foundation of mathematics, providing the core language, concepts and materials for the description and use of numbers, functions and other structures.

As a branch of mathematics, set theory reduces numbers to sets. There are two basic kinds of numbers – ordinals and cardinals. An ordinal number is the answer to: Which one? (first, second, third . . .) A cardinal number is the answer to: How many? (one, two, three . . .) Starting with the empty set, $\{\}$, the set with no members at all (is there only one?), the simplest way of reducing numbers to sets is with this definition of ordinals, due to Zermelo:

$$0 = \{\}$$
$$1 = \{0\}$$
$$2 = \{1\}$$
$$3 = \{2\}$$
$$\cdot$$
$$\cdot$$
$$\cdot$$

Thus, for example, $2 = \{ \{ \{ \} \} \}$. An alternative definition is due to von Neumann, where ordinals are just the set of all ordinals that come before; so $2 = \{0, 1\}$. Then the first infinite ordinal is $\omega = \{0, 1, 2, 3, \ldots\}$, the least number greater than any finite ordinal, the first transfinite number.

Set theory was essentially founded by Georg Cantor in 1874 when he proved that there are different sizes of infinity – distinct and ascending cardinal numbers beyond the finite. By comparing the set of all natural numbers ω to the set of all the real points between 0 and 1, called the linear continuum, Cantor found that the two sets cannot be paired off in a one-to-one correspondence. He proved this with a diagonal argument, which is a recipe for taking collections and constructing some object not in that collection; diagonalization would be used in 1931 by Gödel to prove the incompleteness of arithmetic.

Cantor knew that the size of the linear continuum is greater than the size of ω, and he guessed that it is the next greater size, with no cardinals in between. But Cantor was unable to prove this, and his guess is now known as the continuum hypothesis. The continuum hypothesis is still unresolved; it has been shown that current set theory will never be able to decide whether or not it is true.

Set theory has always generated controversy. Because it reduces numbers to sets, it offers an analysis and explanation of numbers and counting; but some do not endorse this reduction, because they find it artificial or unilluminating. Most importantly, earlier versions of set theory were prone to various paradoxes. For example, consider the set of all cardinals. This set has some size. But for every transfinite cardinal, there is a strictly greater cardinal. So there then must be a greater cardinal than that of the set of all cardinals. This leads directly to a contradiction.

Following the discovery of many such contradictions, leading to widespread talk of a crisis in the foundations of mathematics, set theorists adopted a strict axiomatic method. In 1908 Zermelo developed a set theory in which he was explicit about his assumptions (or axioms). These became known as the Z axioms; and when Fraenkel added one more to the list, the resulting system became known as ZF. When the axiom of choice is added – a point of some disagreement at first – we have the system ZFC, which is today the most widely accepted version of set theory, although there are many alternatives. *See also* CARDINALITY; FOUNDATIONS OF MATHEMATICS; PARADOX; RECURSION; SET; TYPE-THEORY; CANTOR, GEORG. [ZW]

Simplification. *See* INFERENCE, RULES OF.

Soundness. Soundness refers to two different but related concepts in logic.

(1) An *argument* is said to be sound if and only if it is deductively valid and
has only true assumptions. The conclusions of sound inferences are
accordingly guaranteed to be true, although there can be deductively
valid arguments that are not sound, and whose conclusions can be either
true or false. There are two types of sound argument in sense (1), depending on whether the true assumptions of the inference include some merely
logically contingent propositions, or only logically necessary propositions.
These are: (a) materially or contingently sound inferences; (b) logically or
logically necessarily sound inferences. Sound inferences in sense (1a) are
of importance especially in the natural sciences and practical reasoning,
where in contrast (1b) is the sense of primary interest in theoretical logic
and metalogic. Materially or contingently sound inferences are those
inferences involving at least one merely contingently true assumption,
where the remaining assumptions are logically true. Logically or logically
necessary sound inferences are those inferences involving only logically
true assumptions, also known as tautologies or logical theorems.

(2) A *system of logic* is said to be semantically sound if and only if it is both
semantically consistent and semantically complete. A logic is semantically
consistent if and only if it implies only tautologies and deductively valid
inferences, with no inconsistencies, contingent falsehoods or deductive
invalidities among its implications. To be semantically complete, a logic
must imply every tautology and deductively valid inference. Combining
these two requirements, a system of logic is standardly said to be semantically sound if and only if it implies all and only tautologies and deductively
valid inferences. Since tautologies are logical truths or theorems of logic,
it follows that inferences derived from the axioms, definitions and inference rules of any semantically sound system of logic will themselves be
exclusively logically sound arguments in sense (1b).

See also CONTINGENT; FORMAL SYSTEM; TAUTOLOGY; TRUTH; VALIDITY. [DJ]

Square of Opposition. The square of opposition exhibits relationships
between the four forms of categorical proposition. Universal affirmative (*A*)
propositions assert that the subject is wholly within the predicate. Universal
negative (*E*) propositions deny that any of the subject is within the predicate.
Particular affirmative (*I*) propositions assert that at least one member of the
subject is within the predicate. Particular negative (*O*) propositions deny that
all members of the subject are within the predicate. Thus, each has universal

or particular quantity and affirmative or negative quality. In modern notation the four propositions are as follows:

$$A : (\forall x)(Qx \rightarrow Rx)$$
$$E : (\forall x)(Qx \rightarrow \neg Rx)$$
$$I : (\exists x)(Qx \land Rx)$$
$$O : (\exists x)(Qx \land \neg Rx)$$

Pairwise relationships between these propositions comprise a square:

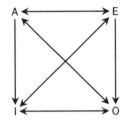

Figure 7 Square of opposition.

A and *O*, and *E* and *I* are *contradictories*: exactly one of each pair is true. Hence the contradictory of a proposition is its negation. Contradiction holds even for empty categories. The other relationships require *existential import*: specifically, the subject must have at least one member. The *contraries A* and *E* cannot both be true, but can both be false, or one of each. The *subcontraries I* and *O* cannot both be false, but can both be true, or one of each. Lastly, each particular proposition is the *subaltern* of the universal of similar quality, its *superaltern*: if the superaltern is true, so is the subaltern; and if the subaltern is false, so is its superaltern.

Categorical propositions may also undergo *conversion*, exchanging subject and predicate, *obversion*, inverting the quality and replacing the predicate by its complement, and *contraposition*, replacing the subject by the complement of the predicate and vice versa. *A* and *O* are equivalent to their contrapositives, *E* and *I* to their converses, and all four to their obverses.

All these relationships originate in Aristotle's *Organon*, although the square itself postdates him. Other squares of opposition, including modal and exponible, may also be derived. *See also* PREDICATE; PROPOSITION; QUANTIFICATION; SYLLOGISM; ARISTOTLE; ORGANON. [AA]

Statement, Compound. A compound (or 'complex', or 'molecular') statement or formula is any statement or formula that is not simple. A compound statement / formula contains at least one logical operator. For example, '¬A' is a compound formula, because it contains the negation symbol, which is a logical operator. *See also* CONNECTIVES; LOGICAL OPERATOR; QUANTIFIER; SENTENCE; STATEMENT, SIMPLE. [SML]

Statement, Simple. A simple (or 'atomic') statement/formula contains no other statement / formula as a part. Thus, it contains no logical operators. For example, in propositional logic an atomic formula is just a propositional variable. *See also* CONNECTIVES; LOGICAL OPERATOR; QUANTIFIER; SENTENCE; STATEMENT, COMPOUND. [SML]

Subcontrary Proposition. *See* SQUARE OF OPPOSITION.

Syllogism. Syllogisms are two-premiss arguments. The usage is typically restricted to deductive arguments, especially those comprised of categorical propositions. Well-formed categorical syllogisms contain exactly three terms, of which a distinct pair occurs in each proposition. The *middle* term occurs in both premisses. The *minor* and *major* terms are respectively the subject and predicate of the conclusion (which gives each term an abbreviation: M, S, P, respectively). Each premiss is named for the term occurring only in that premiss. The major premiss is conventionally stated first. Since categorical propositions have only four logical forms, *A, E, I, O*, syllogisms have 4 × 4 × 4 = 64 combinations of forms, or *moods*. The order of the terms in the premisses can vary, so each mood occurs in 2 × 2 = 4 ways, or *figures*. In the first figure each term occurs in the same place in its premiss as in the conclusion. The second figure switches the terms in the major premiss; the third figure in the minor premiss and the fourth figure in both.

Figure	1	2	3	4
Major premiss	MP	PM	MP	PM
Minor premiss	SM	SM	MS	MS
Conclusion	SP	SP	SP	SP

Hence there are 64 × 4=256 categorical syllogisms. Of these 15 are valid. (24 if all propositions have non-empty subjects.)

AAA1	EAE2	IAI3	AEE4
EAE1	AEE2	AII3	IAI4
AII1	EIO2	OAO3	EIO4
EIO1	AOO2	EIO3	(AEO4)
(AAI1)	(AEO2)	(AAI3)	(EAO4)
(EAO1)	(EAO2)	(EAO3)	(AAI4)

There are several ways of demonstrating the validity of categorical syllogisms. Traditional logic transformed valid syllogisms into canonically valid first figure forms through conversion, obversion and contraposition. The mnemonic names (beginning Barbara, Celarent, for *AAA*1, *EAE*1) record this process: the vowels represent the mood, the initial letter the target first figure syllogism and the consonants the required transformations.

There are lists of rules such that all and only invalid syllogisms break at least one rule. For example:

Rule	Associated fallacy
Syllogisms must have exactly three terms.	Four terms
The middle term must be distributed at least once.	Undistributed middle
Terms distributed in the conclusion must be distributed in the premisses.	Illicit process
At least one premiss must be affirmative	Exclusive premisses
A negative conclusion must follow from a negative premiss	Negative premiss/ affirmative conclusion
A particular conclusion cannot follow from two universal premisses	Existential fallacy

A term is *distributed* when the proposition in which it occurs makes a claim about every member of the class to which it refers. Hence distributed terms are either the subject of universal (A or E) propositions or the predicate of negative (E or O) propositions. Tolerating the existential fallacy admits the nine syllogisms ruled invalid when universals may have empty subjects.

Validity can also be determined diagrammatically. If a three-circle Venn diagram models the relationships expressed in the premisses of a valid syllogism, it must also model the conclusion, which can thus be 'read off' the diagram. Care is required with particular premisses, which may indicate only that either of two regions is non-empty. Not all syllogisms are categorical. The inference rules hypothetical syllogism and disjunctive syllogism inherit names traditionally given to two-premiss deductive arguments containing implications or disjunctions respectively. *See also* INFERENCE, RULES OF; PROPOSITION; PRACTICAL SYLLOGISM; SQUARE OF OPPOSITION; VENN DIAGRAMS; ORGANON. [AA]

Syntax. Providing the syntax of a formal theory is the first step in its construction. The syntax consists of the language, or alphabet, in which the theory is written, along with rules for constructing well-formed formulae. Syntax is opposed to semantics, which governs the assignment of truth-values to those formulae. *See also* SEMANTICS. [RM]

Tableau. *See* SEMANTIC TREE.

Tautology. A tautology is a statement that is true by virtue of its form and cannot, therefore, be false. The term is defined formally in propositional logic, as a formula that is true under all possible interpretations of its propositional variables. For example, the proposition $p \lor \neg p$, called the law of excluded middle, is a tautology in classical logic. To test whether a proposition is a tautology, we can use truth-tables. The negation of a tautology is called a contradiction. *See also* CONTRADICTION; LAW OF EXCLUDED MIDDLE; LOGIC, PROPOSITIONAL; TRUTH-TABLES. [DH]

Theorem. A theorem of a theory T is a statement ϕ that can be derived from the axioms of T using the rules of inference of T. More precisely, if T is a formal system, then ϕ is a theorem if and only if there exists a proof in T whose last formula is ϕ. *See also* AXIOM; INFERENCE; INFERENCE, RULES OF; FORMAL SYSTEM; PROOF; SENTENCE. [NK]

Theorems. Generally speaking, in mathematical logic, theorems are well-formed formulae that can be proved using previously accepted rules or axioms. A proof consists of a series of statements that are in accordance with the rules or axioms, and it is possible to have several different proofs of the same theorem. Of philosophical interest are some very famous theorems that have been highly influential in the development of logic, mathematics and scientific thought. A few of them are discussed below.

Löwenheim-Skolem Theorem. Around the beginning of the twentieth century, logicians and mathematicians were working on the foundations of mathematics. Russell, Zermelo and others were working on the idea that mathematics could be reduced to logic; Hilbert proposed that mathematics could be formalized and that this formal system together with a proof of its consistency would provide a foundation for mathematics. One of the problems that arose was that the formulae comprising the language have many possible interpretations and so the question arose as to whether all these models were the ones expected, or were there unintended interpretations that were at odds with known results? For example, informally, if we think of the natural numbers and how we might categorize them, using only symbols and formulae in logic, we need to be sure those symbols and formulae do not have interpretations or models outside of the domain of natural numbers.

Löwenheim (1915) and Skolem (1920) were able to show that unintended interpretations do exist and the resulting theorem, the proof of which is highly mathematical, is known as the Löwenheim-Skolem Theorem. The work of Löwenheim and Skolem gave birth to the extremely productive branch of mathematical logic called model theory, an accessible introduction of which is to be found in Badesa, Calixto's (2004), *The Birth of Model Theory: Löwenheim's Theorem in the Frame of the Theory of Relatives* (Princeton, NJ: Princeton University Press).

Gödel's Theorems. Kurt Gödel proved several far-reaching theorems, which have been tremendously influential in mathematical, scientific and philosophical endeavour since the 1930s. Gödel is particularly famous for his two incompleteness proofs. Informally, the first incompleteness theorem tells us that if we have a consistent theory of arithmetic, it cannot also be complete; in other words, within our theory, we can construct a true statement of arithmetic that we cannot prove. The second incompleteness theorem tells us that if we have a formal theory, or set of axioms, of arithmetic together with some accepted truths about provability, then, if the theory is consistent, it cannot prove its own consistency.

Gödel made many other contributions to logic, including a proof that the continuum hypothesis cannot be disproved using the axioms of set theory, if those axioms are consistent. Gödel also made significant advances in proof theory, wherein proofs are themselves analysed as mathematical objects. See for example, Nagel, E. and Newman, J.R. (eds). 2001. *Gödel's Proof.* New York: New York University Press; Smith, P. 2007. *An Introduction to Gödel's Theorems.* Cambridge: Cambridge University Press. *See also* MODEL THEORY; PROOF THEORY; THEOREMS; GÖDEL, KURT. [DH]

Theory. A theory Δ is a logically closed set of sentences of a formal language L: Let 'Cn' denote the operation of logical consequence defined on L; then, Δ is a theory if and only if $\Delta=Cn(\Delta)$, where $Cn(\Delta)$ is the set of the logical consequences of Δ. When Δ doesn't contain contradictions, we say that Δ is a consistent theory. *See also* CONSISTENCY; CONTRADICTION; DEDUCTION; LOGICAL CONSEQUENCE; SENTENCE; SET; TARSKI, ALFRED. [GC]

Truth. There are two main difficulties with the concept of truth. The first has to do with the consistency of the concept of truth while the second has to do with the nature of truth.

The concept of truth is notoriously involved in paradoxes. Consider the sentence 'This sentence is not true': if it's true then it's not, and if it's not then it is (Liar paradox). Or one might consider sentences like 'If this sentence is true, then A' and prove that A (Curry's paradox). One obtains a related paradox by considering the adjectival phrase 'not true of itself' and ask whether it's true of itself (Grelling paradox). Those paradoxes have long been thought to cast serious doubts on the legitimacy of the concept of truth. Answers to the paradoxes are possible however. In this respect the philosophical and logical import of Tarski's 'The concept of truth in formalized languages' (1933. The concept of truth in formalized languages. In *Logic, Semantics, Metamathematics, papers from 1923 to 1938* (1983. ed. Corcoran, J., Indianapolis: Hackett Publishing Company) can hardly be overestimated.

Tarski's theory proceeds in two steps. First, Tarski offers an analysis of our concept of truth. The crucial remark here is that each instance of the following T-schema can be regarded as a partial definition of truth in a language L, one which captures soberingly our basic intuition that truth consists in some correspondence to the facts:

(T-schema) S is true if and only if p

where 'S' must be replaced by a name of a sentence of L and 'p' by an appropriate translation of it. This analysis allows for the formulation of an adequacy condition (Convention-T): any candidate definition (or theory) of truth for a language L should have as consequences the infinite lot of T-sentences (instances of the T-schema).

Then Tarski proceeds to show that a consistent, though limited, use of the truth-predicate is made possible by keeping distinct the language containing the truth-predicate (the metalanguage) and the language to which it applies (the object language). More specifically, Tarski proves that the set of true sentences of an exactly specified, interpreted language L can be adequately defined in a metalanguage. To do so, it is enough that the metalanguage be built out of the object language by adding to it a theory of morphology (e.g. a kind of arithmetic dealing with strings of L instead of numbers) and some logical framework which must be 'essentially richer' than the one available in the object language (e.g. being higher order). The possibility of defining explicitly the set of true sentences of L in a logically (and arithmetically) enriched metalanguage amounts to a consistency proof of the restricted truth-concept (relative to the consistency of the concepts of logic and arithmetic, supposed to be unproblematic). This significant result had the effect of rehabilitating the concept of truth among suspicious philosophers and of clarifying the principled distinction between truth and provability.

After Tarski, one major focus of subsequent research has been to overcome the limitation of this early result and show that a language may also consistently contain its own truth-predicate (Kripke, S. 1975. Outline of a theory of truth. *Journal of Philosophy*, 72(19): 690–719; Gupta, A. 1982. Truth and paradox. *Journal of Philosophical Logic*, 11: 1–60; Hintikka, J. 1998. *The Principles of Mathematics Revisited*, Cambridge University Press; H. Field, *Saving Truth from Paradox*, Oxford University Press, 2008, among others).

In general, theories addressing the question of the consistency of truth are neutral regarding the question of the nature of truth (albeit this is sometimes debated). We now come to the latter problem and briefly discuss the four main competing accounts of the nature of truth in the modern philosophical debate: pragmatic truth, coherence truth, correspondence or classical truth and deflationist truth.

On the pragmatic accounts (e.g. of James, Pierce), there is nothing more to truth than what is useful to believe. While on the coherence account (e.g. Blanschard, Bradley), to be true is just to fit coherently in a set of (systematic, justified) beliefs. The basic insight behind those two theories is this: since we have no direct access to unconceptualized facts, there can be no better criteria for truth attribution to a proposition, in the last analysis, than its fitting best, be it in terms of usefulness or coherence, in our conceptual scheme. Pragmatic and coherence accounts, however, have mostly been discarded today. The reason is that they seem to be incompatible with the fact that it is central to our understanding of the concept of truth that we know a priori that:

It is true that snow is white if and only if snow is white.

For certainly it is not true a priori that:

It is useful to believe that snow is white if and only if snow is white.

or that

It is coherent to believe that snow is white if and only if snow is white.

This is not to say that there isn't something right to the pragmatic and coherence insights (they may have other problems however, most notably with falsehood), but rather that they are better construed as pertaining, not to the notion of truth, but to the epistemic theory of justification.

By contrast, correspondence and deflationist theories firmly stick to the analyticity in 'true' of the T-sentences. Both theories can be said to capture the 'correspondence intuition', however the correspondence theorist is further committed to the view that these sentences hold in virtue of a certain robust relation obtaining between sentences and the world, or facts etc. The existence of a genuine relation is the bulk of the correspondence theory of truth, and it is its task to explain further what this relation is. Nevertheless, we might deny that that there is anything to be explained. This is the deflationists' position. The reason is that, deflationists argue, 'true' is just an internal, logical device: it is convenient to assert some infinite lot of sentences ('All first-order Peano axioms are true') or to endorse blindly some other's utterances ('Plato's last sentence is true'), and for this reason 'true' is not dispensable, but it does not stand for any real substantial property, one that might have some causal/explanatory power.

Issues to adjudicate the debate range from philosophy of logic to meaning theories, meta-ethics and general methodological questions in philosophy. *See also* METALANGUAGE; PARADOX; TRUTH-MAKER; VALIDITY; TARSKI, ALFRED. [HG]

Truth-Table. A truth-table is a tabular representation of the truth-value of a compound statement of propositional logic, given the truth-values of its atomic formulae. Each row of the table represents a possible assignment of truth-values to the atomic formulae; each column represents the possible truth-values of either the compound statement or its atomic formulae. The truth-tables for ¬*A*, *A*∨*B*, *A*∧*B*, *A*→*B*, *A*↔*B* are given below (the letters T and F stand for the truth-values true and false, respectively).

A	¬*A*
T	F
F	T

A	B	A∨B	A∧B	A→B	A↔B
T	T	T	T	T	T
T	F	T	F	F	F
F	T	T	F	T	F
F	F	F	F	T	T

A truth-table is an effective way of computing the truth-value of every statement of propositional logic; truth-tables provide an algorithm for deciding
whether a given statement of propositional logic is valid, that is whether its
truth-value is T for every row of the table. The number of different truth-
tables and the number of their rows depend on the number of different
atomic formulae occurring in the table. In the case of 2 different atomic
formulae there are 16 different truth-tables with 4 rows; each of them
corresponds to a different binary connective. Although truth-tables originated
in classical logic, which recognizes only the two truth-values true and false,
truth-tables can be extended to multi-valued logic.

Early attempts to use truth-tables date back to the late years of nineteenth
century. Peirce, Schröder and Dodgson (better known as Lewis Carroll) are
credited with the original development of truth-tables. Emil Post made use
of truth-tables in his proof of completeness of propositional logic in 1920.
The adoption of truth-tables became widespread after the publication of
Wittgenstein's Tractatus (1921), in which truth-tables played a crucial role.
See also CONNECTIVES; LOGIC, MULTI-VALUED; LOGIC, PROPOSITIONAL; TRUTH-VALUE; VALIDITY;
PIERCE, CHARLES SANDERS; WITTGENSTEIN, LUDWIG; TRACTATUS. [MMu]

Truth-Functional. An adjective most frequently applied to (some) connectives. A truth-functional connective satisfies the following condition: for an
n-place connective and *n* truth-values, one can compute the truth-value
of the connective on the basis of the truth-value(s) plugged in. That is, the
value of the whole expression is based solely on the truth value(s) of its
parts. One needn't have any other information. This is not always the
case. '___ because___' has no determinate truth-value based solely on
the truth-values of its blanks. '___ and___' is truth-functional, however.
'Truth-functional logic' refers to logical systems containing truth-functional
connectives and no quantifiers. *See also* CONJUNCTION; CONNECTIVES; QUANTIFIER;
TRUTH-VALUE. [CF]

Truth-Maker. A truth-maker is an entity by virtue of whose existence a truth-bearer (a proposition) becomes true: 'Socrates died' is true in virtue of the event of Socrates' death, 'Peter is clever' is true in virtue of Peter's cleverness and 'Tigers are carnivorous' is true in virtue of the kind universal tiger being characterized by the property universal carnivority. One truth-maker can often make several truth-bearers true (e.g. both 'Socrates died' and 'Xanthippe's husband died'); and one truth-bearer can sometimes be made true by several different truth-makers (e.g. 'There is at least one number dividable by three' is made true by each such number). See also CATEGORY; PROPOSITION; TRUTH. [LJ]

Truth-Value. Traditionally, propositions have one of two possible truth-values: true and false. So, 'Birds fly' has the truth-value 'true' and 'Fish knit' has the truth-value 'false'. Only propositions (not questions, commands or exclamations) have truth-values. The truth-value of a proposition is one of its semantic properties. See also BIVALENCE; EXCLUDED MIDDLE, LAW OF; PROPOSITION; SEMANTICS; TRUTH. [APM]

Turing Machine. An abstract machine defined by Turing in 1936 in order to investigate the properties of computable functions. It consists of an infinite tape divided in cells containing the symbols 0 or 1; the machine can read and write every cell, moving the tape one cell at a time. A set of instructions, represented as a table of transition rules for the machine's states, determines its behaviour. Turing proved the existence of a universal Turing machine that can simulate every Turing machine. The problem of determining whether a Turing machine will halt on a given input (halting problem) is not decidable. See also COMPUTABILITY; DECIDABILITY; TURING, ALAN. [MMu]

Type Theory. Type theory originated as a solution to a family of formal logical, semantic and set theoretical paradoxes. The theory was first advanced as a component of the classical formal logical system known as the predicate or functional calculus, developed by Alfred North Whitehead and Bertrand Russell, in the *Principia Mathematica* (1910–1913; Cambridge University Press, 2nd edn. 1925).

Russell's paradox, discovered in 1901, defines a set *R* as the set of all sets that are members of themselves, and a set *R'* as the set of all sets that are not members of themselves. Together, the two definitions logically imply the contradiction that *R'* is a member of *R* if and only if *R'* is not a member of *R*.

To avoid such antinomies, Russell assigns all syntax items a particular index or order number. Object terms, constants or names and object variables, referring to individual things, belong to order 0; predicates representing the properties of 0-order objects are of order 1 (thus, standard predicate logic is also known as first-order logic); predicates representing the properties of 1-order properties are of order 2 and so on, indefinitely. Russell then restricts the formation principles in the typed logic in such a way that only predicates of order $n+1$ can attach to a predicate or object term of order n in a well-formed formula.

The limitation effectively precludes as improperly formulated any syntactical combination of terms T1 and T2 such that $T1^n(T2^n)$ (asserting that term T1 is true of term T2), permitting only such constructions as $T1^{n+1}(T2^n)$. The restriction avoids Russell's paradox along with other explicit logical and formal semantic paradoxes by prohibiting the original definitions of R and R' from being properly formulated in a typed logic. *See also* CLASSES; LOGIC, N-ORDER; PARADOX; RUSSELL'S PROGRAMME; SET THEORY; PRINCIPIA MATHEMATICA. [DJ]

Universal Generalization. *See* QUANTIFICATION RULES.

Universal Instantiation. *See* QUANTIFICATION RULES.

Universal Quantifier. A logical operator in predicate logic, which indicates that something is true of every object in the domain. It takes the form of 'For all x', and is symbolized by (x), or $\forall x$. So (x) $(Qx \rightarrow Rx)$ translates as 'For all x, if x is Q then x is R.' *See also* DOMAIN; EXISTENTIAL QUANTIFIER; LOGIC, PREDICATE; LOGICAL OPERATOR; QUANTIFIER. [ML]

Universe of Discourse. The collection of objects that form the subject matter of an investigation. In a formal system, it is the collection of objects over which the individual variables range and, consequently, can be distinct from the domain. In geometry, for instance, the universe of discourse includes shapes, planes, points etc. *See also* DOMAIN; INTERPRETATION; QUANTIFICATION; VARIABLE. [AH]

Use / Mention. Consider (1) 'Jim is short'. Initially, there are two plausible readings of (1): one where the subject is a word and another where it's a person. When speaking, we can say 'The word "Jim" is short', but we can be more economical in print. Placing quotes around a word yields a name for that word, enabling us to speak about (mention) it. So, ' "Jim" is short' talks about the word 'Jim' while (1) talks about a person (by using the name). Clarity of expression is especially important in philosophy, where we may just as readily talk about words or objects. *See also* DE RE / DE DICTO. [CF]

Validity. Validity is a property of an argument or an inference. Generally and informally, we say that an argument or inference is valid if its premises provide some degree of support for its conclusion. Different notions of validity correspond to different strengths of support that premises might supply to a conclusion.

For instance, an argument or inference is said to be deductively valid if the truth of its premises *guarantees* the truth of its conclusion; in other words, in every possible circumstance in which the premises are true, the conclusion is also true. Thus, validity is a semantic notion. Given a particular formal theory *T*, we say that an argument or inference in *T* is valid if, in all models of *T* in which the premises are true, the conclusion is also true. Or, equivalently, an argument or inference in *T* is valid if the set of sentences consisting of its premises together with the negation of its conclusion is inconsistent: that is, there is no model in which they are all true.

By defining validity in this way, we introduce a pathology. If the premises of our argument or inference are inconsistent, then the argument is valid no matter what the conclusion is. This is often summarized by saying that from a contradiction one can infer anything.

However, it seems that deductive validity is not the only variety of validity, for it seems that the premises of an argument or inference can support its conclusion without guaranteeing its truth. For instance, the following argument seems to be valid, but it is clearly not deductively valid:

> Very few extant mammals lay eggs.
> Veronica is a mammal.
> Therefore, Veronica does not lay eggs.

So it seems that there is a notion of validity that is weaker than deductive validity: we call it inductive validity. There are a number of ways of making this notion precise, and each leads to a different sort of inductive logic. For instance, we might say that an argument or inference is inductively valid if the premises make the conclusion *likely* or *probable*. This definition leads to probabilistic logic. Or we might say that an argument is inductively valid if, in all *normal* circumstances in which the premises are true, the conclusion is true. This leads to nonmonotonic logic. *See also* ARGUMENT; FORMAL SYSTEM; INDUCTION; INFERENCE; LOGIC; LOGIC, INDUCTIVE; LOGIC, NONMONOTONIC; LOGIC, PROBABILISTIC; MODEL; THEORY; VALIDITY; VALIDITY, INDIRECT TEST FOR. [RP]

Validity, Indirect Test of. Consider this propositional argument: $\varphi_1, \ldots, \varphi_n$; therefore, ψ. Here is the direct test for its validity:

(D1) Produce a joint truth table for $\varphi_1, \ldots, \varphi_n, \psi$.
(D2) Consider each row on which each of $\varphi_1, \ldots, \varphi_n$ are true.
(D3) If there is such a row on which ψ is false, the argument is invalid. Otherwise, valid.

Sometimes it is quicker to use the indirect test for validity:

(ID1) Produce a joint truth-table for $\varphi_1, \ldots, \varphi_n, \psi$.
(ID2) Consider each row on which ψ is false.
(ID3) If there is such a row on which $\varphi_1, \ldots, \varphi_n$ are all true, the argument is invalid. Otherwise, valid.

See also ARGUMENT; LOGIC, PROPOSITIONAL; TRUTH-TABLE; VALIDITY. [RP]

Variable. Variables in formal systems function similarly to pronouns in natural language; their reference varies. In 'A → ¬B', 'A' and 'B' are propositional variables, which stand for sentences, or propositions. In the predicate logic formula ' ∃x(Qx ∧ Rx)', 'x' is a variable, which stands for an object, or name of an object. Higher order logics also contain variables in predicate positions.
See also PREDICATE; PROPOSITIONAL VARIABLE; QUANTIFIER. [RM]

Venn Diagrams. A diagrammatic scheme first published by John Venn in 1880 as an improvement over Euler diagrams. Instead of representing the actual relationships between the classes involved in an argument, Venn represents first all their possible combinations. For instance, two intersecting circles show the four possible sub-classes (*x y*, *x* not-*y*, not-*x y*, not-*x* not-*y*) of two given classes *x* and *y*. Then one adds visual devices to indicate the state of the sub-classes. In modern use, a cross (or '1') represents the existence of a class while shading (or '0') indicates its emptiness. A not-marked class is indefinite.

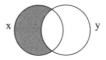

Figure 8 All *x* are *y*.

Figure 9 No x is y.

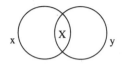

Figure 10 Some x are y.

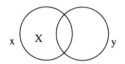

Figure 11 Some x are not y.

See also EULER DIAGRAMS; VENN, JOHN. [AM]

Verisimilitude. Verisimilitude is similarity to the whole truth. A sentence or theory is highly verisimilar if it says many things and many of these things are true. This means that the verisimilitude of a theory depends both on its informative content (how much the theory says) and on its accuracy (how much of what the theory says is true). Suppose that, in a very simple language, $A \wedge B \wedge C$ is the maximally informative true description of the world. Consider then the following examples:

1. The sentences A and $\neg B$ are equally informative, since both make a 'single claim' about the world; however, A is true, and then more verisimilar than $\neg B$, which is false.
2. The sentences A and $A \wedge B$ are equally accurate, since all they say is true; however, $A \wedge B$ is more informative, and then more verisimilar, than A.

The latter example also shows that verisimilitude is different from probability: in fact, $A \wedge B$ is less probable, although more verisimilar, than A. The first formal definition of verisimilitude was proposed by Popper, K. (1963. *Conjectures and Refutations*, Routledge). Afterwards, the problem of verisimilitude has been investigated by Oddie, G. (1986. *Likeness to the Truth*. Dordrecht: Reidel), Niiniluoto, I. (1987. *Truthlikeness*. Boston: Reidel), Kuipers, T. (1987.

What is Closer-to-the-Truth?. Amsterdam: Rodopi) and many others. For a survey, see Oddie, G. (2007. 'Truthlikeness', *The Stanford Encyclopaedia of Philosophy*). *See also* LOGICAL CONSEQUENCE; POSSIBLE WORLD; PROBABILITY; SENTENCE; THEORY; TRUTH. [GC]

Key Thinkers

Abelard, Peter. Peter Abelard (Latin: Petrus Abaelardus or Abailard) (1079–1142) was a French medieval philosopher, theologian and logician. Abelard can be considered the father of Scholasticism, the medieval manner of philosophizing that aimed to ground Christian doctrine on the logical rigour of dialectical reasoning. In his commentaries on Aristotle, Porphyry and Boethius and in his large logic treatise (the four books of the 'Dialectica') he formulated a conceptualist solution to the problem of universals (according to which properties intended as single entities literally shared by many individuals only exist in the human mind), provided a thorough study of syllogism, and emphasized the role of propositions (rather than terms) in language and logic, developing a purely truth-functional propositional logic based on the notion of 'inferentia' (i.e., of entailment between premises and conclusion). Moreover, Abelard introduced the de re / de dicto distinction that differentiates two types of modal statements, and is said to have been the first to recognize the Fregean distinction between the force and the content of a sentence. [MMo]

Aristotle. Aristotle (384/3BC–322BC) was a Greek philosopher and scientist, the first to formulate logic as a general theory of inference. His logical works are assembled in the *Organon* and have the titles of *Categories, On Interpretation, Prior Analytics, Posterior Analytics, Topics* and *On Sophistical Refutations*.

The *Categories* deal with notions that are said without any combination, for example: Socrates, horse, high, beautiful. Categories are the fundamental elements of being, and from the logical standpoint are the highest genera. There are ten categories: (1) substance; (2) quantity; (3) quality; (4) relation; (5) place; (6) time; (7) posture; (8) habit; (9) action; (10) passion. The first and most important is substance, for without it no other categories could be predicated.

In *On Interpretation*, Aristotle deals with the theory of proposition, in which the subject is combined with a predicate. In this book, Aristotle asserts the identity of language, thought and reality. The two necessary elements of a proposition are noun and verb and only in their combination is there truth and falsity. Truth is accordance with reality, while falsity is disagreement with reality. Aristotle provides also a first sketch of modal logic by introducing the notions of possibility, existence and necessity.

In *Prior Analytics*, Aristotle develops the theory of logical inference. The most important logical inference is the syllogism, namely an inference composed by three propositions, in which the conclusion is inferred from two premisses of a certain form. For example: All animals are mortal (major premise), all men are animals (minor premise), all men are mortal. The second kind of inference dealt by Aristotle is confutation, which proves the contrary of the conclusion by showing that a contradiction follows from the premisses. The third kind is induction, which infers from particular premisses a general conclusion. Induction has no demonstrative value; it has only heuristic value, aiming towards new knowledge. The last kind is abduction, in which the major premise is true, the minor is probable or not demonstrable, and therefore the conclusion is not certain. An example of abductive inference is: The body is a mortal thing, the soul is an immortal thing, the soul survives the body.

The *Posterior Analytics* deal with scientific or demonstrative syllogism, which is a particular kind of syllogism that has always true premisses, from which always true conclusions derive. In the second book of the *Posterior Analytics*, Aristotle explains how to obtain universal knowledge by means of sensation, memory and experience.

The *Topics* deal with dialectical arguments, which have opinions as premisses. Dialectical arguments must not be confused with the eristic arguments dealt with in *On Sophistical Refutation*, whose aim is not to discover truth, but to merely dispute. The premisses of dialectical inferences are opinions accepted either by all or by the majority or by wise men, and have therefore an epistemological value for Aristotle.

In the *Metaphysics*, Aristotle elaborates for the first time the principle of non-contradiction, which says that one cannot say of something that it is and that it is not, in the same respect and at the same time. The ontological formulation of principle of non-contradiction states that it is impossible for one thing to be and to not be at the same time. From the principle of non-contradiction follows the principle of the excluded middle, which asserts that there cannot be an intermediate between contradictories, but of one subject we must either affirm or deny any one predicate.

Aristotle deals in *Rhetoric* and *Poetics* with the art of the rhetorical and poetical discourse. Rhetoric is the art of the persuasion and its logical argument is the enthymeme. The enthymeme is a syllogism that proceeds from probable premises and its aim is to convince the audience and not to find the truth. Poetics deals with imitation of human actions by means of language, rhythm, verses and harmony. The main logical argument of the poetics is the example, which is a kind of incomplete induction that produces a general concept capable of capturing all the characteristics of its particular instances. [MS]

Arnauld, Antoine. Antoine Arnauld (1612–1694) was a French priest, theologian and philosopher. He was the principal author of *La logique, ou l'art de penser*, better known as the Port-Royal Logic, perhaps the most influential of early modern logic texts. Arnauld was a prominent exponent of Jansenism, a controversial movement in seventeenth century French catholicism inspired by the Dutch bishop Cornelius Jansenius (1585–1638). Jansenists emphasized personal spirituality and divine grace over free will, echoing Calvinist thought, but defying mainstream catholicism. The formerly Cistercian convent of Port Royal, where Arnauld's sister Angélique (1591–1661) was abbess, became a stronghold of Jansenist thought. Some of Arnauld's best-known works were composed as contributions to its educational programme.

In addition to his many works of theological controversy, Arnauld was a prolific philosopher. His philosophical works include *General and Rational Grammar* and the fourth set of objections to Descartes's *Meditations*. The former work, otherwise known as the Port-Royal Grammar, was a companion to the *Logic*, with which it shared a strong Cartesian influence. It has been credited by Noam Chomsky with anticipating some of his own work in linguistics. [AA]

Barcan Marcus, Ruth. Ruth Barcan Marcus (b. 1921) developed quantified modal logic in the 1940s. She is known for the Barcan formulae and for the Barcan proof of the necessity of identity. [SML]

Bayes, Thomas. Thomas Bayes (ca. 1702–1761) was a British Presbyterian minister, theologian and logician. His 'Essay towards solving a problem in the doctrine of chances' (1764) – published posthumously by his friend Richard Price in the *Philosophical Transactions of the Royal Society of London* – contains the statement of a special case of what is known today as Bayes' theorem. In the essay, Bayes deals with the chance of events in connection to pre-existing circumstances and after the occurrence of particular events – which he termed 'prior odds' (or probability) and 'posterior odds', respectively. Bayes proposes that evidence confirms the likelihood of a hypothesis only to the degree that the evidence would be more probable with the assumption of the hypothesis than without it. Although his name is nowadays connected to a number of interpretations of probability that share the idea that probabilities express degrees of beliefs rather than frequencies, it remains unclear whether Bayes himself would have endorsed such an understanding or, instead, put more emphasis on observable entities and events. [MMo]

Bolzano, Bernard. Bolzano's thought on logic, mathematics and philosophy is now recognized to have anticipated much better known later works. His posthumously published *Paradoxes of the Infinite* (1852) was the most sophisticated treatise on infinite sets before Cantor. His four volume *Theory of Science* contains detailed thoughts on truth, propositions and logical consequence, all developed because Bolzano did not believe that logic at the time was adequate for use in mathematics. These were well in advance of Tarski's semantic conception of logical consequence.

For Bolzano, logic was broadly conceived to include epistemology, metaphysics and philosophy of science. Rebuffing any intrusion of psychology, like Frege to come, Bolzano was concerned with logic objectively, 'on its own' – writing of propositions, ideas and truth in themselves.

A priest and professor of Catholic doctrine in Prague, Bolzano's life included philanthropy and controversy. His work was noticed by Husserl and Twardowski. To date he is best remembered for the Bolzano-Weierstrass theorem of calculus (that every bounded infinite set of reals has an accumulation point), but his other accomplishments are increasingly becoming appreciated. [ZW]

Boole, George. George Boole (1815–1864) was an English mathematician, philosopher and the inventor of Boolean algebra. He was born on 2 November 1815, into a working-class family in the English city of Lincoln.

His first paper, published at the age of 24 was: 'Researches in the theory of analytical transformations, with a special application to the reduction of the general equation of the second order' printed in the *Cambridge Mathematical Journal* in February 1840. For this work he received, in 1844, a gold medal from the Royal Society and an honorary degree of LL.D. from the University of Dublin.

A prolific author and contributor to the burgeoning theory of differential equations, Boole is, however, best known for his work in logic. He invented Boolean algebra, expounding his thoughts initially in his 1847 book, *The Mathematical Analysis of Logic*. His ideas on reasoning and his logical system were developed further in 'An Investigation on the Laws of Thought on which are founded the Mathematical Theories of Logic and Probabilities' 1854. This, his most famous work, is usually referred to simply as Boole's *Laws of Thought*. Boole was appointed the first Professor of Mathematics, Queen's College, Cork, Ireland in 1849, where he devoted the rest of his life to academic study.

Boolean operators are used in search engines; next time you use Google or AltaVista, remember Boole; it is through his work that we have the options AND, OR, EOR (exclusive OR, also symbolized as XOR) and NOT. For example, 'true OR true' returns 'true' but (true XOR true) returns 'false' since XOR only allows only one of the statements to be true; not both. Boole's work on the algebra that bears his name proved to be fundamental to the design of digital computer circuits, where 'true' and 'false' are denoted by 1 and 0, respectively. From the additional operators, NAND (NOT AND) and NOR (NOT OR), all the others can be built.

Boole was made a Fellow of the Royal Society in 1857. Tragically, seven years later, on 8 December 1864, he died of pneumonia in Ballintemple, County Cork, Ireland. He is buried in Blackrock, a suburb of Cork. The Moon crater Boole is named in his honour. [DH]

Bradwardine, Thomas. Thomas Bradwardine (c. 1300–1349) published work in philosophy, mathematics and theology. His focus in logic was the insolubles such as the liar paradox: 'What I am saying is false'. His solution accepts that this sentence is false, but not that it is true. He rejects that P implies that 'P' is true. In order to establish that 'P' is true we need to show that everything it signifies is the case – but we cannot do this. His approach influenced many later accounts (such as those of Buridan and Albert of Saxony). [CA]

Brouwer, Luitzen Egbertus Jan. Luitzen Egbertus Jan Brouwer (1881–1966), or 'Bertus' to his friends, was a Dutch mathematician who made a number of noteworthy mathematical discoveries in topology (a branch of geometry) and whose views within the philosophy of mathematics have been extremely influential. He is the founder of a school of thought known as intuitionism – the view that the truth of mathematical statements is not independent of our thought. Brouwer's motivations for developing this position were philosophical, and can be traced back to his 1905 book *Life, Art and Mysticism*. With clear Kantian and Schopenhauerian overtones, he contends there that real thought is a kind of non-intellectual and non-linguistic mental experience. In his 1907 dissertation *On the Foundations of Mathematics* Brouwer applied these ideas to mathematics. He argued that mathematical truths are grounded in real thought (i.e. experience) alone. Two things follow from this: (1) There are no unexperienced mathematical truths, and so no realm of independently existing mathematical objects (i.e. Platonism is false). (2) Mathematical truths are non-linguistic and so any attempt to ground mathematics in linguistic axioms must fail (i.e. Formalism is false). Brouwer continued to develop this position right up until his last publication in 1955. [BC]

Buridan, Jean. Jean Buridan (ca 1300–1358) was a fourteenth-century French logician and philosopher. In his textbook, *Summulae de dialectica*, one of the strongest influences on logic through the early modern period, Buridan discussed all of the standard topics of medieval logic: syncategorematic terms (logical constants), supposition theory (reference), insolubles (semantic paradoxes), syllogisms, and fallacies. [SU]

Cantor, Georg. The German mathematician Georg Cantor (1845–1918) is the founder of modern set theory. Prior to his work, mathematicians had been using an implicit, naive concept of set without a distinction between different sizes of infinite sets. Cantor proved that the set of real numbers is 'bigger' than the set of natural numbers, showing for the first time that there exist infinite sets of different sizes.

Cantor clarified the concept of an infinite set with his distinction between cardinal and ordinal numbers, on which he built an arithmetic of infinite sets. He showed that there are infinitely many possible sizes for infinite sets. He also introduced the concept of the power set of a set A, which is the set of all possible subsets of A, and he proved what became known as Cantor's theorem: the size of the power set of A is strictly larger than the size of A, even for an infinite set A.

Cantor also introduced the continuum hypothesis, which states: 'There is no set whose size is strictly between the set of the integers and the set of the real numbers.' Kurt Gödel and Paul Cohen proved the hypothesis to be independent from the axioms of ZFC set theory. [KV]

Carnap, Rudolf. Rudolf Carnap (1891–1970) was one of the leading members of the Vienna Circle, a group of philosophers whose position is known as Logical Positivism or Logical Empiricism.

Carnap studied logic with Frege, and wrote two introductions to symbolic logic, *Abriss der Logistik* (1929) and *Einführung in die symbolische Logik* (1954). Carnap's technical contributions to formal logic are interesting but rather unfortunate. At the end of the 1920s, he worked on a flawed (and only recently published) manuscript 'Investigations to general axiomatics', in which he tried to clarify the notions of consistency, completeness and categoricity. Gödel managed to get the notions clear, and this led to his famous incompleteness proof. This proof was a serious blow for logicism, of which Carnap was a major exponent. In *Meaning and Necessity* (1947), he elaborated the first semantical models for modal logics by means of the method of intension and extension, but this work was soon eclipsed by Kripke's possible worlds semantics.

Carnap is especially famous for his philosophical applications of the new logic. On his recommendation, the Viennese circle around Moritz Schlick took an interest in logic, and sought to combine logic with a strong empiricist epistemology. Carnap's *Der logische Aufbau der Welt* (1928) is the most notable elaboration of this logical-empiricist project. He tried to provide a precise and formal redescription of all knowledge on the basis of logic and one extra-logical predicate (recollection of similarity) only.

Carnap's physicalism implies that all scientific theories in the natural sciences should be expressed in a formal logical language. Hence, in his semantical works *Logische Syntax der Sprache* (1934), *Introduction to Semantics* (1942), *Formalisation of Logic* (1943) and *Meaning and Necessity* (1947), he studied the syntactic and semantic features of various formal languages. Carnap believed that logical (and mathematical) statements can be unequivocally distinguished from descriptive statements, a view later contested by Quine in his attack on the analytic-synthetic distinction. Since the 1950s, Carnap worked on inductive logics and their application to scientific confirmation. [LD]

Carroll, Lewis. Pen name of Charles L. Dodgson (1832–1898). British logician better known for his widely quoted 'Alice' tales. He published *The Game of Logic* (1886) and *Symbolic Logic: Part 1* (1896). Fragments of *Part 2* appeared in 1977. He invented rectilinear diagrams for solving syllogisms and pioneered the use of trees to test the validity of sorites. He is best remembered for two papers in the journal *Mind*, 'A logical paradox' (1894) and 'What the Tortoise said to Achilles' (1895). The latter is often considered as the best exposition of the difference between a premise and a rule of inference. [AM]

Chomsky, Noam. Noam Chomsky's (b. 1928) investigations of natural language syntax resulted in the nested 'Chomsky hierarchy' of grammar types (unrestricted, context-sensitive, context-free and regular). Chomsky also advocated a grammatical level of logical form to represent scope and other contributions to semantics attributable to principles of universal grammar. [ABr]

Chrysippus. The Greek philosopher Chrysippus of Soli (280–206 B.C.) was one of the founders of Stoicism. A pioneer of propositional logic, he has been credited with the first account of disjunction.

Although Chrysippus was a prolific author, none of his works survive: his views must be reconstructed from commentary by his critics. His lasting memorial may be 'Chrysippus's Dog', a thought experiment concerning the logical capacities of animals. Imagine a dog tracing a scent to a crossroads, sniffing all but one of the exits, and then proceeding down the last without further examination. According to Sextus Empiricus, Chrysippus argued that the dog effectively employs disjunctive syllogism, concluding that since the quarry left no trace on the other paths, it must have taken the last. The story has been retold many times, with at least four different morals:

1. dogs use logic, so they are as clever as humans;
2. dogs use logic, so using logic is nothing special;
3. dogs reason well enough without logic;
4. dogs reason better for not having logic.

The third position is perhaps Chrysippus's own.

A legend of Chrysippus's death continues the animal theme: he is said to have died laughing as a drunken donkey tried to eat figs. [AA]

Church, Alonzo. In 1936, Alonzo Church, Emil Post and Alan Turing each proposed independent explications of the informal notion of an effectively computable function, or algorithm. The three formal notions were later shown to select the same class of mathematical functions. Further equivalent formulations have been produced by Gödel and others. The resulting thesis, that the computable functions are the recursive functions, has become known as Church's Thesis, or the Church-Turing thesis. (The notion of a recursive function traces to Gödel; Church considered a related class of functions called λ-definable.)

Church's Thesis is important because we want to know whether some problems have algorithmic solutions. For example, Church initially formulated the thesis in an attempt to answer the question of whether first-order logic was decidable. A theory is decidable if there is a procedure for determining whether any given formula is a theorem. Since recursion is formally definable, Church's Thesis provides a method for determining whether a particular problem has an effective solution. It provides a formal characterization of an intuitive concept.

Church's Thesis is also important because of its relation to Turing's formulation. Turing selected the recursive functions by considering the abilities of logical computing machines, or Turing Machines. Some writers who have compared Turing machines to human minds have used Church's Thesis with excessive enthusiasm, making broader claims about its implications than are supported by the thesis properly construed. In fact, Church's Thesis is entirely silent about the nature and limitations of both the human mind and computing machines.

Church's Thesis is widely accepted. It appears that every recursive function is effectively computable, and it also appears that every effectively computable function is recursive. Still, there is some debate over whether Church's Thesis is provable. This debate has focused on whether any identification of an informal concept with a formal notion can be proven. Some philosophers consider Church's Thesis to be a working hypothesis. Others take it to be merely another mathematical refinement of a commonsense notion like set, function, limit or logical consequence.

Church's Thesis is independent of the purely technical result called Church's Theorem. Church's Theorem shows that first-order logic is recursively unde-cidable, as long as it contains non-monadic predicates. (A monadic predicate, like 'is blue', takes only one argument, in contrast to relational predicates, like 'is bigger than' or 'is between'.) Appending Church's Thesis to Church's Theorem, as Church did, we can show that there is no effective decision procedure for first-order logic, no sure method for deciding whether a formula of first-order logic is valid. However, there is a decision procedure for monadic predicate logic. [RM]

De Morgan, Augustus. British mathematician and logician (1806–1871), he published two major books: *Formal Logic* (1847) and *Syllabus of a Proposed System of Logic* (1860), together with a series of five papers 'On the Syllogisms' (1846–1862) which contains the bulk of his contributions to logic. De Morgan's early works are mainly remembered for the priority dispute that opposed him to the Scottish philosopher Sir William Hamilton (1788–1856) on the quantification of the predicate, although both were actually preceded by the botanist George Bentham (1800–1884) who already introduced that idea as early as 1827. This innovation was thought of highly at the time; the quarrel brought a considerable publicity to the study of logic and turned out to be influential as it stimulated George Boole's early logical investigations.

From a logical viewpoint, the quantification of the predicate increased the number of propositional forms (eight instead of the four traditional A, E, I, O propositions) and consequently the list of valid and invalid syllogisms. As such, it illustrates De Morgan's efforts to reform and extend the logic of his time. The admission of negative terms (such as 'not-*X*') is another instance of his desire to go beyond traditional syllogisms. De Morgan's most important contribution in this direction, however, is the introduction of relations in the field of logic, with the treatment of new forms of statements ('*A* is greater than *B*') and inferences ('man is animal, therefore the head of a man is the head of an animal') which were outside the syllogistic tradition.

De Morgan and Boole are often associated as being the founders of 'mathematical logic' (an expression coined by De Morgan). Hi treatment is less alegebraic than Boole's however. In a way, De Morgan acted as a reformer of traditional logic and opened the way to Boole's more radical changes. Although most of De Morgan's contributions to logic are now outdated, two of his innovations are still widely used: the rules related to the negation of conjunctions and disjunctions (widely known as the Laws of De Morgan) and the concept of the universe of discourse. [AM]

Frege, Gottlob. Gottlob Frege (1848–1925) was a German mathematician, logician and philosopher whose invention of quantificational theory inaugurated modern logic, and who – together with Bertrand Russell, G. E. Moore and Ludwig Wittgenstein – was one of the main founders of analytic philosophy. Born in Wismar in northern Germany, he studied mathematics, physics, chemistry and philosophy at the Universities of Jena and Göttingen from 1869 to 1873, and taught mathematics at Jena from 1874 until he retired in 1918.

The three books that he published in his lifetime were *Begriffsschrift* (Conceptual Notation) in 1879, *Die Grundlagen der Arithmetik* (The Foundations of Arithmetic) in 1884 and *Grundgesetze der Arithmetik* (Basic Laws of Arithmetic), the first volume of which appeared in 1893 and the second volume in 1903. Frege's main aim in these books was to demonstrate the logicist thesis that arithmetic is reducible to logic. In *Begriffsschrift* he gave his first exposition of the logical system by means of which arithmetic was to be reduced. In *Grundlagen* he offered an informal account of his logicist project, criticizing other views about arithmetic, such as those of Kant and Mill. In *Grundgesetze* he refined his logical system and attempted to demonstrate formally his logicist thesis. In 1902, however, as the second volume was going to press, he received a letter from Bertrand Russell informing him of a contradiction in his system – the contradiction we know now as Russell's paradox. Although Frege hastily wrote an appendix attempting to respond to the paradox, he soon realized that the response did not work, and was led to abandon his logicist project. He continued to develop his philosophical ideas, however, and to correspond with other mathematicians and philosophers, and published a number of influential papers.

The central idea of Frege's logicism is the claim that a number statement involves an assertion about a concept. To say that Jupiter has four moons, for example, is to say that the concept *moon of Jupiter* has four instances, something that can be defined purely logically. The significance of this idea comes out when we consider negative existential statements (a type of number statement, involving the number 0), such as 'Unicorns do not exist'. We might be tempted to construe this as attributing to unicorns the property of non-existence. But if there are no unicorns, then how is this possible? On Frege's view, however, the statement is to be interpreted as 'The concept *unicorn* has no instances', which makes clear that there is no mysterious reference to unicorns themselves, only to the *concept* of a unicorn. The general strategy here, reformulating a potentially misleading proposition to reveal its 'real' logical form, was to become a central idea of analytic philosophy.

Besides his books, Frege is best known for three papers he wrote in the early 1890s, 'Function and Concept', 'On Sense and Reference' and 'On Concept and Object', and a series of three papers he published under the general title of 'Logical Investigations' in 1918–1923, of which the most famous is 'Thought'. In the first set of papers Frege outlines the main ideas that informed the development of his logical system – his use of function-argument analysis, the doctrine that concepts are functions that map objects (as arguments) onto truth-values, the distinction between concept and object, and the distinction between sense (*Sinn*) and reference (*Bedeutung*). The latter is the most well known of all Frege's ideas, introduced in order to explain how identity statements can be both correct and informative. According to Frege, an identity statement such as 'The morning star is the evening star' is correct because the two names 'the morning star' and 'the evening star' have the same reference, namely, the planet Venus, and informative because the two names nevertheless have different senses – reflecting the different ways in which Venus is presented (as seen in the morning and as seen in the evening). In Frege's later paper 'The Thought', he develops his ideas further, explaining how 'thoughts' (as the senses of sentences) can be regarded as inhabiting a 'third realm' distinct from both the physical and the mental realms.

Frege's ideas had a huge influence on Russell and Wittgenstein, and through them on the development of analytic philosophy, especially in the areas of philosophy of language, logic and mind. In recent years, even Frege's philosophy of mathematics has been given a new lease of life by so-called neo-logicists, who have attempted to bypass the problems caused by Russell's paradox. Frege's ideas are more vigorously debated now than at any point in the past. [MB]

Gödel, Kurt. Kurt Gödel (1906–1978) was a seminal figure in mathematical logic. Born in Brünn, Moravia, Gödel received a Ph.D. in 1930 from the University of Vienna. After Austria was annexed by Germany, he and his wife Adele emigrated to Princeton, where he was a member of the Institute for Advance Study and where he remained until his death.

Among Gödel's many achievements are consistency proofs for both the Axiom of Choice and the Generalized Continuum Hypothesis with the other axioms of set theory, and also a relative consistency proof of arithmetic. Only his most famous results, Completeness and Incompleteness, are discussed here.

Completeness of First Order Axiomatic Systems. In 1930 Gödel published his dissertation, proving the completeness of first-order logic.

The Completeness Theorem states that for every proposition A in a (classical) first-order axiomatic system, either there is some interpretation of the system in which A is true or there is a proof of $\neg A$ in that system. This means that every first-order tautology has a proof in first-order logic. Another consequence is that given a classical first-order system, we can always determine its consistency or inconsistency. If it is consistent, then it has an interpretation that is either finite or denumerable. If it is inconsistent, then there is a finite proof of a contradiction in that system. Part of the significance of the Incompleteness Theorems is that they show that there are important systems for which these criteria do not hold.

The Incompleteness Theorems. In 1931 Gödel published the Incompleteness Theorems in 'On Formally Undecidable Propositions of *Principia Mathematica* and Related Systems I'. Both theorems apply to axiomatic systems, such as that developed by Russell and Whitehead in the *Principia Mathematica*, that contain a certain amount of elementary arithmetic and that use methods of reasoning known as 'finitary'. Consider such a system S.

The First Incompleteness Theorem states that there are undecidable propositions in S. A proposition A is said to be undecidable if A is a well-formed formula in the language of S, but neither A nor $\neg A$ is provable in S. A is of the form $\forall(x)F(x)$, where F is a well-defined predicate. That is, A makes a claim about whether a certain, clearly defined property holds for all of the natural numbers. Such a property holds for all of the natural numbers or it does not, but S itself cannot produce a proof one way or the other.

The Second Incompleteness Theorem states that, if S is indeed consistent, some propositions expressing the consistency of S are undecidable. In other words, a proof that S is consistent requires inferences that cannot be formalized in S itself.

These theorems have had a wide influence on the development of mathematical logic. For instance, they show that the modes of reasoning envisioned by Hilbert to establish the veracity of mathematics are not sufficient to do so. They have also stimulated large swaths of research in various sub-disciplines of mathematical logic. [AH]

Hilbert, David. David Hilbert (1862–1943) was the progenitor of metatheory in logic and mathematics. He was among the most prominent mathematicians of his time. His achievements in mathematics include work on geometry, number theory, algebra and analysis; he also contributed to the theory of relativity. Hilbert shaped the direction of mathematical thought in the twentieth century, most famously by framing the Paris Problems: 23 open questions presented at the 1900 International Congress of Mathematicians.

In philosophy of mathematics, Hilbert is variously characterized as a formalist and as a finitist. While Hilbert's views contain elements of both formalism and finitism, neither of these terms effectively captures the subtlety of his thought. Some formalists hold that mathematical theories are best understood as uninterpreted systems. Some finitists reject all infinitary results. In contrast, Hilbert believed both that some mathematical statements were true of real objects and that transfinite mathematics was legitimate.

In the early twentieth century, philosophers of mathematics struggled to understand the ramifications of various oddities of set theory, including Cantor's paradox (arising from consideration of the set of all sets), the Burali-Forti paradox (arising from consideration of the well-ordering of the ordinals), and Russell's paradox (arising from the assumption that every property determines a set). Intuitionists, for example, Brouwer, concluded that the infinitary mathematics which leads to these paradoxes was illegitimate. Hilbert, in contrast, wished to establish finitistic foundations for infinitary mathematics.

Hilbert distinguished between real and ideal mathematical formulae. Real formulae are generally finitistic, and may be directly verified. Mathematical theories which included ideal elements were instead to be tested for their consistency. Unlike logicists like Frege, for whom the consistency of mathematics follows from the presumed truth of its axioms, Hilbert took the consistency of a set of axioms as sufficient evidence for mathematical legitimacy. Further, Hilbert took ideal formulae to be meaningless. Hilbert's emphasis on consistency and his claims about the meanings of ideal formulae have led people to consider him a formalist.

In addition to consistency, if one can show completeness, that every valid theorem is provable, then one could hope for a solution to all open mathematical problems. Hilbert tried to establish that mathematical theories were both consistent and complete by studying mathematical systems themselves. He thus founded the metamathematics and metalogic that characterize much of contemporary logical research.

Many logical theories are provably consistent and complete. In contrast, Gödel's incompleteness theorems struck a decisive blow against Hilbert's pursuit of these results for mathematics. Gödel's first theorem showed that, for even quite weak mathematical theories, a consistent theory could not be complete. Gödel's second theorem proved that the consistency of a theory could never be proven within the theory itself. We can only prove that mathematical theories are consistent relative to other theories.

Hilbert's views survive in Hartry Field's fictionalism, which emphasizes the consistency of mathematical theories; in Mark Balaguer's plenitudinous platonism, which asserts that every consistent mathematical theory truly describes a mathematical realm; and in defenses of limited versions of Hilbert's Programme. [RM]

Jeffrey, Richard. Philosopher and logician. A former student of Carnap and Hempel, he is best known for his theory of 'probability kinematics' – a form of belief revision that explains how an agent can change her beliefs when she receives uncertain evidence – and his development of an evidence-based version of Decision Theory. [AWS]

Jevons, William S. William Stanley Jevons (1835–1882) was a British logician and economist who developed and refined the propositional calculus of George Boole. He eliminated the confused features of Boole's system, such as the inverse operations of subtraction and division, and established the convention of reading 'or' as inclusive disjunction. He is also remembered for his invention in 1869 of the 'logical piano', a mechanical device which could determine the relationships of consistency between propositions. As one of the first to automate logical inference, Jevons may be seen as a forerunner of modern computer science. [AA]

Kripke, Saul Aaron. Kripke (b. 1940) is a renowned philosopher and logician who has published well-known and highly influential work in modal logic, the philosophies of logic and language, metaphysics and the philosophy of mind, and who has written an important book on some themes addressed in Wittgenstein's later work (1982. *Wittgenstein on Rules and Private Language*. Oxford: Blackwell).

Between 1959 and 1965 Kripke published pivotal work in modal logic, especially concerning the provision of a model-theoretic semantics for modal logic (see, e.g. 1963: Semantical considerations on modal logic. *Acta Philosophica Fennica*, 16: 83–93; reprinted 1971 in Leonard Linsky (ed.), *Reference and Modality*. Oxford: Oxford University Press, 63–72). Kripke defines a model-structure (for systems at least as strong as T: see Logic, Normal-Modal) as follows:

'A model-structure . . . is an ordered triple (**G**, **K**, **R**) where **K** is a set, **R** is a reflexive relation on **K**, and **G** $\in$ **K**. Intuitively, we look at matters thus: **K** is the set of all "possible worlds"; **G** is the "real world". If H_1 and H_2 are two worlds, H_1RH_2 means intuitively that H_2 is "possible relative to" H_1; i.e. that every proposition *true* in H_2 is *possible* in H_1.' (1971, 64).

R is commonly known as 'the accessibility relation'. Kripke (1963/1971) uses this definition of a model-structure to define a model for propositional modal logic and a model for quantified modal logic. Intuitively, a statement is necessary at a world if and only if it is true at all possible worlds accessible from the world of evaluation. Kripke's approach enables the relationships between different systems of modal logic to be specified in terms of the properties of **R** within those systems (rather than, as previously, in terms of the characteristic axioms of the systems).

In 1970 Kripke gave three lectures at Princeton University which were later published as (1972. 'Naming and necessity'. In Davidson, D. and Harman, G. (eds), *Semantics of Natural Language*. Dordrecht: Reidel, 253–355; 1980: *Naming and Necessity*. Oxford: Blackwell). This is probably the most influential work in analytic philosophy since 1960. Despite the central appeal to possible worlds in this and earlier work, Kripke (1980: 14–20, 44) is not (unlike, e.g., David Lewis) a realist about possible worlds. Kripke defends both a direct reference account of proper names (siding with Mill against Frege and Russell) and the view that proper names are rigid designators.

Kripke also launches an attack on the thesis that a truth is necessary if and only if it is a priori, claiming that there are necessary a posteriori truths and suggesting, more tentatively, that there are contingent a priori truths. He defends the thesis of the necessity of identity and employs it against versions of materialism in the philosophy of mind held to entail that mental states are contingently identical to brain states.

Kripke (1975. 'Outline of a theory of truth'. *Journal of Philosophy*, 72(19): 690–719) offers an original (and technically demanding) approach to the semantic paradoxes. [SML]

Leibniz, Gottfried Wilhelm. Leibniz, Gottfried Wilhelm (1646–1716) was a German philosopher, mathematician and logician, and arguably the founder of mathematical logic. Leibniz's logicism, as read by Bertrand Russell, had much impact upon early Anglo-Saxon analytic philosophy.

Leibniz's logic is symbolic and aims at reducing all logical arguments to a combination of signs. For instance, denoting with the letter *a* the category of substance, the letter *b* the category of quantity, the letter *c* the category of quality and combining the substance with man, the quantity with tallness and the quality with beauty, the sentence 'beautiful man' corresponds to *ac*, the sentence 'tall man' corresponds to *ab*, and the sentence 'beautiful tall man' to *abc*.

Logic is therefore grounded on calculus, where the design of a good notation is fundamental for the representation of human reasoning. Leibniz experiments with numerous notations aiming at the algebraic treatment of relations. But he also conceives of logic in a much broader sense than the modern view he is often called to legitimize. In calculus, every concept would have a corresponding sign, a suitable character that represents it. The combination of signs would ideally bring about a universal language, which ought to account for all concepts and their combinations. Combining concepts, then, is one of the tools Leibniz uses to set up his *ars combinatoria* that would make possible the acquisition of new truths as well as their rigorous proof.

Leibniz clarifies the conceptual distinction between necessity and contingency, dividing all truths into two kinds: truths of reason and truths of fact. The former are necessary so that their negation is impossible. The latter are contingent and their opposite is possible. Truths of reason do not derive from sensible experience, for they are founded solely on the principle of identity, and thus on the principle of non-contradiction. Truths of reason are all mathematical demonstrations.

Truths of fact derive from experience and the negation of their conclusion is conceivable without contradiction. They are based on the principle of sufficient reason, which says that there must be a sufficient reason for anything to exist, for any event to occur, for any truth to obtain. Nothing happens without a reason. The facts of nature are guided by the actual infinite, so that the root of contingency lies in the infinite. Truths of fact could become truths of reason, that is, necessary truths only by means of an infinite analysis but the latter would surpass the theoretical resources of any human epistemic agent.

Analysis provides for clear and distinct cognition. On the intensity of clarity and distinctness is based the difference between sensitive and intellectual cognition. Intellectual cognition is clearer and more distinct than sensitive cognition. However, analysis requires different modes of representation, notations and diagrams which include irreducible visual aspects. On the other hand, the difference between the two is not absolute, it is instead graded, for gradation is nothing more than the expression of the law of continuity, which says that nature makes no leaps. The third principle enunciated by Leibniz is the principle of the identity of indiscernibles, which states that two or more objects or entities are identical if and only if they have all properties in common. [MS]

Leśniewski, Stanisław. Leśniewski (1886–1939), Polish logician and philosopher, established the Warsaw School of Logic together with Łukasiewicz. He proposed a system of logic intended as a most general description of reality. Leśniewski's logic consists of Prototethic (generalized propositional calculus), Ontology (calculus of objects) and Mereology (calculus of mereological or collective classes). [NB]

Lewis, Clarence Irving. American philosopher (1883–1964) with pragmatist leanings, Lewis criticized the handling of material implication in Russell and Whitehead's *Principia Mathematica* in 'Implication and the logic of algebra' (*Mind*, 1912). Instead, in 'The calculus of strict implication' (*Mind*, 1913), he proposed a 'strict implication' with ramifications for formal modal languages. His idea of the 'pragmatic a priori' contrasts necessary truths with contingent facts by claiming the former are indispensable to theory, rather than that they cannot be thought without contradiction. [KD]

Lewis, David Kellogg. Lewis (1941–2001) was an eminent, versatile and prolific American philosopher. Lewis (1973. *Counterfactuals*. Oxford: Blackwell) offers a semantics for counterfactual conditionals. On the account of Robert Stalnaker (1968. A theory of conditionals. In Rescher, N. (ed.), *Studies in Logical Theory*. Oxford: Blackwell, 98–112), a counterfactual conditional is true if in the possible world most similar to the actual world in which the antecedent is true, the consequent is true. For example, 'If I had asked Elaine to marry me she would have refused' is true if among those possible worlds in which I did ask Elaine to marry me the possible world most similar to the actual world is one in which she refused.

In addressing de re modality, Lewis (1973, 39–43; 1986: *On the Plurality of Worlds*. Oxford: Blackwell) invokes 'counterpart theory'. I am not agnostic, but, according to Lewis, I might have been since there is another possible world in which there is a counterpart of me who is in fact agnostic. Counterparthood is a relation of similarity rather than identity: I exist only in the actual world. In our example, the counterfactual is true at the actual world, w^*, if there is a world, j, closely similar to w^*, in which my counterpart asks Elaine's counterpart to marry him and she refuses and there is no world, k, such that k is at least as similar to w^* as is j and at k my counterpart proposes to Elaine's counterpart and she does not refuse (after 1973, 42).

Lewis (1986) defends counterpart theory, realism about possible worlds and the view that modal operators are quantifiers over possible worlds.

Lewis (1991. *Parts of Classes*. Oxford: Blackwell) provides an original contribution to the philosophy of set theory. [SML]

Lindenbaum, Adolf. Lindenbaum (1904–1941), a distinguished member of the Warsaw School of Logic, had a central part in the development of metamathematics. Best known are the Lindenbaum maximalization lemma and Lindenbaum-Tarski algebra. He had important results in the foundations of set theory, especially the axiom of choice, and in multi-valued logic. [NB]

Löwenheim, Leopold. Löwenheim (1878–1957) is known for his work on relations and for an early provocative result in logic, which has come to be known as the Löwenheim-Skolem theorem. The theorem says that if a first-order theory requires models of infinite size, models can be constructed of any infinite size. [RM]

Łukasiewicz, Jan. Łukasiewicz (1878–1956), the leader of the Warsaw School of Logic, had important results within propositional logic, the most prominent being the discovery of multi-valued logic. He made revolutionary contributions to the history of logic, particularly ancient Greek logic. Łukasiewicz also invented a bracket-free logical symbolism known as Polish notation. [NB]

MacColl, Hugh. Scottish logician (1837–1909). He is remembered for introducing propositional calculus in the late 1870s and modalities in the late 1890s. He later collected his innovations in *Symbolic Logic and its Applications* (1906). His theory anticipated C. I. Lewis's work on implication and opened the way to pluralism in logic. [AM]

Megarians. The Megarian School was founded in Athens by Eucleides of Megara (c.435–c.365) in the first half of the fourth century BC. Eucleides, a student of Socrates, combined Parmenides' notions of oneness and immutability with Socrates' idea of true knowledge. The sensible world of perceptions is said to be an illusion, so that the essential natures of things are 'bodiless forms'. Eucleides defends the unity of goodness: while the highest good accounts for the highest reality, the opposite of goodness has no existence. Eubulides of Miletus, successor of Eucleides, criticized Aristotle's concepts of motion and potentiality, which endanger the unity of goodness. Indeed, change contradicts immutability; and potentiality conflicts with oneness, insofar as not all potentialities are actualized. The fact that not all possibilities are realized allows a multiplicity of opposites to be possible.

Diodorus Cronus, who had some influence on Stoic logic, assumed that what is possible about the past is necessarily realized in the present or future. He defined the so-called Master Argument, based on the three following assertions:

(1) Everything true about the past is true in the present.
(2) The impossible does not follow from the possible.
(3) Something that is possible may never be true (i.e. may never be realized).

The third proposition is said to be false, and is thereby inconsistent with the two other true assertions. Diodorus defended the view that all possibilities are realizable in the present or future, meaning that whatever is possible is actual at some time. Thus, what is possible either is, or will be, true. By contrast, Philo of Megara, student of Diodorus, held the view that not all possibilities are realizable, as he supposed that the future does not contain the realizations of all possibilities. What is possible may not be actual at some future time; that is, not all possible events will be actualized. In that case, what is possible may be false.

The Megarians were the first to coin the Liar paradox, namely: If we say that we are lying, are we telling the truth or are we lying? They also adopt the *eristic* method, which aims to win arguments, contrary to Socrates' *heuristic* method whose purpose is to discover truths in reality. Eristic is often associated with *sophistic* in relation to arguments that systematically refute everything incompatible with the defended doctrine. [JLH]

Mill, John Stuart. John Stuart Mill (1806–1873) was an English philosopher and economist, whose father James Mill belonged to the Scottish school of psychology. An extremely precocious and gifted child, he was educated by his father in a very rigorous way, according to the principles of Jeremy Bentham, his godfather and the founder of utilitarianism. As intended by his father, he became a fervent spokesman for utilitarianism, whose principle is that in promoting pleasure one increases social welfare. But at age 19 he experienced a 'crisis of his psychological history', a deep nervous breakdown caused by his too strict education. It made him realize that the principles of utilitarianism must be made more humanistic, as he would later argue in his 1863 *Utilitarianism*. From 1823 to 1858, he was an administrator in the East India Company. His ambition of becoming a 'master in democracy' led him to be a liberal MP in 1865. He spent most of the end of his life in Provence where his wife was buried.

Though his interests were in great part political, he won his philosophical spurs not only with the *Principles of Political Economy*, but also with his fundamental *System of Logic* in 1843. He later expressed his conceptions about logic and reasoning in *An Examination of Sir William Hamilton's Philosophy* and in the notes to the edition of his father's *Analysis of the Phenomena of the Human Mind*.

Mill's system was criticized by modern logicians (such as Jevons, Peirce and Frege) for representing empiricism or psychologism in logic. He indeed views logic as a branch of psychology, differing from it in dealing only with valid reasoning and in being an art rather than a science. Lately, this disparaging judgment has been reconsidered by supporters of naturalism who hold that regulative processes emerge from the growth of natural entities.

Mill's main point is that the propositions and inferences of logic have a genuine cognitive content: they do not state analytical truths but empirical facts about the world. Even mathematics is an empirical science, which cannot be known a priori. It challenges what he calls 'intuitionism' (e.g. Kantian thought), a position holding that one can know something about the world in·only studying our mind's structure.

One of Mill's major advances is to have drawn from his empirical stance the conclusion that the province of logic includes not only deductive syllogism, but scientific reasoning in general. He assumes that scientific method is inductive (which would make him Popper's favourite target), and therefore provides a complete study of what makes an induction valid.

During his lifetime, Mill's central opponent regarding induction was William Whewell, who claimed that a general proposition cannot be a mere juxtaposition of discrete cases, but requires a general conception to be added in order to 'colligate' the facts. On the other hand Mill's position implies that generality is nothing but an accumulation of particulars. [JMC]

Ockham. William of Ockham (c. 1287–1347/9) was an English scholastic philosopher. He was a pioneer of nominalism, arguing that only individuals exist, and denying the existence of metaphysical universals. According to Ockham, a universal such as redness is the result of abstraction by the human mind from individual red things. As such, they have no extra-mental existence. Ockham also placed a general emphasis on reducing one's ontology to the bare minimum, as reflected in the methodological principle that has come to be known as 'Ockham's Razor' (or 'Occam's Razor', based on the Latinized form of his name): 'in vain is done with more what can be done with fewer'. This principle is often expressed using the slogan, 'Do not multiply entities beyond necessity', although it should be noted that this formulation appears nowhere in Ockham's own writings.

In addition to his work on metaphysics, Ockham also made significant contributions to mediaeval logic, especially concerning the notions of signification, connotation and supposition. In his *Summa of Logic*, Ockham described logic as 'the most useful tool of all the arts'. [ABa]

Pascal, Blaise. Blaise Pascal (1623–1662) was a French mathematician, physicist and religious philosopher. In mathematics, he wrote on conic sections (1640), designed a calculating device counting integers (1642–1644), laid the foundations for the calculus of probabilities, and interpreted geometry as the ideal scientific method (*Fsprit de géométric*, 1654). In physics, he tested the theories of Galileo and Torricelli by constructing a mercury barometer, and wrote treatises on the weight and density of air. He also invented the syringe, created the hydraulic press and demonstrated, against Aristotle, that a vacuum could exist in nature (1647–1648).

At the end of 1654, Pascal experienced a mystical conversion, and frequented the Jansenist convent of Port-Royal. He had some influence on the writing of the *Logique de Port-Royal* by Arnauld and Nicole. In *Les Provinciales* (1657), Pascal defended Arnauld, on trial for his controversial religious works against the Jesuits. Subsequently, he started his work of Christian spirituality, which remained unfinished at his death; the fragments were published under the title *Pensées* (Thoughts). He argued that a man without Grace was incapable of truth, meaning that only religion had to be loved. Pascal's wager was suggested as an argument for overcoming the indifference of the sceptic. The crucial assumption was that reason was powerless to deduce God's existence; in other words, Descartes' deductive proof was irrelevant. However, reason showed that we could wager on God's existence, for there was nothing to lose and everything to gain. If God did not exist, the sceptic lost nothing but a false belief, which was a finite loss. On the other hand, if God did exist, then the sceptic gained eternal life, which was an infinite gain. The wager from reason was intended only to convince the non-believer, and had eventually to be replaced by faith, that is, love from the heart. [JLH]

Peano, Giuseppe. Giuseppe Peano (1858–1932) was an Italian mathematician who worked at the University of Turin. He devised a set of axioms for arithmetic, known as the Peano axioms, and developed mathematical logic.

When Peano began his research, there was a curious asymmetry between arithmetic and geometry. Geometry had been developed as an axiomatic-deductive system since ancient Greek times (Euclid), but there were no axioms for arithmetic.

Peano tried to remedy this situation in his 1889 work: *Arithmetices principia nova methodo exposita*. His axioms for arithmetic stated informally are the following:

(P1) 1 is a number.
(P2) The successor of any number is a number.
(P3) Two numbers are equal if and only if their successors are equal.
(P4) 1 is not the successor of any number.
(P5) If 1 has the property Q, and if, whenever n has the property Q, its successor n+1 has the property Q, then all numbers have the property Q.

P5, the most complicated of the axioms, is known as the principle of mathematical induction.

We have stated the Peano axioms informally, but this is not in the spirit of Peano himself. He wanted to develop arithmetic as a purely formal axiomatic-deductive system. This meant that no ordinary language would be used and everything would be written in formulae. To achieve this, all the logical principles used in the deduction of theorems from the axioms had to be spelled out as formulae. Peano carried out this task, and, in so doing, developed mathematical logic. Many of the notations he introduced are still used today. For example, he wrote: 'if A, then B' as 'A $\supset$ B', and employed the Spanish tilde ~ to mean 'not'.

Peano and his followers went on, between 1895 and 1908, to present the whole of mathematics as a vast formal system. [DG]

Peirce, Charles Sanders. An American philosopher (1839–1914) who coined the term 'pragmatism' and its associated maxim of ascertaining the meanings of concepts from the consequences of employing them. A pioneer in semiotics – the theory of signs and signification – Peirce also initiated the use of a number of basic methods in modern logic, including truth tables and inclusive, instead of exclusive, disjunction, the treatment of relations as classes of ordered pairs, ordered triplets, and by extension, ordered n-tuples.

Logic – particularly the logic of relations – forms the basis for Peirce's work in semiotics, which adopts a triadic notion of signifier, signified and (ideal) observer; it justified his ongoing search for metaphysical Categories, inspired by Kant; and its employment as a rigorous method in Duns Scotus and Ockham is a paradigm for Peirce's own inquiries into the fixation of belief.

Keen to explicate the contrast between inductive and deductive forms, Peirce distinguished a third type of inference – 'abduction' (or 'retroduction') – which by its very nature is not formalizable and is today often associated with inference to the best explanation.

Like Frege, Peirce held an essentially antipsychologistic view of logic, but also held that logical thought could be normatively subsumed under an aesthetic category of what is ultimately 'satisfactory'. [KD]

Prior, Arthur Norman. Prior (1914–1969) is the founder of modern temporal logic. In his major books *Time and Modality* (1957) and *Past, Present and Future* (1967), he explores the relations between time and logic, and develops a calculus with two 'modal' operators for past and future tenses. [AM]

Quine, Willard Van Orman. Willard Van Orman Quine (1908–2000) studied mathematics in Oberlin College (Ohio), and wrote a Ph.D. thesis in philosophy, 'The Logic of Sequences. A Generalization of Principia Mathematica' (1932), under the supervision of A.N. Whitehead in Harvard, later published as *A System of Logistic* (1934). In 1933, he visited Europe and participated in the meetings of the Vienna Circle, had many discussions with Carnap in Prague, especially on Carnap's manuscript of *Logische Syntax der Sprache* (1934), and met the Polish school of logicians in Warsaw. Until the early 1950s, Quine worked almost exclusively on mathematical logic. In later years, after some groundbreaking philosophical publications such as 'On what there is' (1948), 'Two dogmas of empiricism' (1951) and *Word and Object* (1960), he published mainly in ontology, epistemology and the philosophy of language.

Quine's most remarkable contribution to mathematical logic is his set-theoretic system NF ('New foundations for mathematical logic', 1937). Quine transformed Principia Mathematica (PM)'s grammatical criterion of well-formed ('stratified') formulae into an axiom schema for set admissibility, and thus replaced PM's layered universe by a single universe. The resulting axiom system NF is rather odd: the axiom of choice is not valid, NF contains non-Cantorian sets, that is, sets that can be placed in a one-to-one correspondence with their subsets, and it is counterintuitive to prove theorems in NF. In *Mathematical Logic* (1940), Quine added proper classes to NF, thus obtaining the set-theoretic system ML. Quine's later handbook for set theory, *Set Theory and its Logic* (1963) contains an interesting comparison of various set-theoretic systems, but by that time ZFC was generally accepted as the appropriate axiomatization of set theory.

Quine was a great advocate of first-order logic. In his early work, he clearly separated set theory from the less problematic first-order logic. He argued against 'deviant' logics, such as intuitionistic logic, quantum logic and second-order logic. More importantly, he became the most outspoken critic of the budding modal logic. Quine's negative reaction to Carnap's study of intensional models for modal logic in *Meaning and Necessity* (Carnap, R. 1947. *Meaning and Necessity*. Chicago: University of Chicago Press) was the start of a lifelong campaign against modal logic.

Quine's philosophical work in ontology, philosophy of language and epistemology was deeply influenced by his background in logic. First, ontological issues can only be determined within a logical framework, as the criterion of ontological commitment 'to be is to be the value of a variable' makes clear. Only objects that can be the values of variables bound by the existential quantifier exist. Also set-theoretic technicalities have been important for Quine's ontology. Quine's 'ontological' solution to Russell's paradox was the very basis of his interest in ontology. Second, in *Word and Object*, Quine was one of the first to integrate mathematical logic and natural language. Quine's dismissal of linguistic notions such as meaning and synonymy goes hand in hand with his extensionalism in logic. Finally, Quine's epistemology is strongly influenced by Carnap's logico-philosophical work. His famous rejection of the analytic-synthetic distinction can only be understood against the backdrop of early developments in model theory. Furthermore, inspired by Carnap's *Der logische Aufbau der Welt* (1928), Quine describes the ultimate epistemological aim as the construction of a unified scientific theory expressed in the language of first-order logic. [LD]

Russell, Bertrand. Bertrand Russell (1872–1970) was a British logician-mathematician, philosopher and writer, and one of the founders of mathematical logic. Mathematics and logic provided much of the inspiration for Russell's philosophical development, in particular, the transition from his early neo-Hegelianism and idealist background to his realism which he defended along with G.E. Moore. It was not only questions on the foundation of pure mathematics that inspired Russell's philosophical development. The philosophical transition from idealism to realism is particularly marked in the context of applied mathematics: by the time Russell composes *The Principles of Mathematics* (1903), E. Mach and H. Hertz's research in mechanics prompts an important change in Russell's epistemology. Russell required a perfect language and it is Russell's philosophy of language that establishes the link between his realism and epistemology.

In his early Hegelian phase (1894–1898) Russell was concerned with 'a complete dialectic of the sciences' assuming that all sciences depend on some abstraction that sooner or later leads to contradiction. In 1895 Cantor discovered that to speak of the system of all numbers as a set leads to contradictions. By 1896 Russell learned about Cantor's work and worried about contradictions in connection with the concept of number. He feared that almost all mathematical ideas are infected by contradictions reducible to the paradox of the 'the number of all numbers'.

Russell learned the new logic from Peano in 1900 and enriched it with his own contributions. He developed the full polyadic predicate calculus after he learned Peano's notation and the insights that underlie it. Also called the 'logic of relations', this is one of Russell's most significant contributions to logic which was influenced by his study of Leibniz and arguably also of Peirce's work on logical relations which, in turn, was based on Boole's algebra.

Russell first outlines his logicism in *The Principles of Mathematics* (1903): his idea was to identify numbers with classes of classes so as to frame number-theoretic statements in the vocabulary of quantifiers and identity. This work was unsettled by the discovery of a contradiction in set theory. Frege had been working on logicism too. Russell observed that Frege's attempt to define number by means of classes also generates a contradiction, as the expression 'the class of all classes' could be formulated in the system and if we then ask 'Is "the class of all classes not members of themselves" a member of itself?', we run into contradiction.

Russell's response to the problem of such paradoxes crystallized in the construction of a logical system in which all of the contradictions would be uniformly avoided. The solution comes with his simple theory of types further developed as 'ramified theory' in 'Mathematical Logic as Based on the Theory of Types' (1908) and in the volumes of *Principia Mathematica* (1910–1913), co-authored with Whitehead.

In his original version of the 'paradox' Russell spoke of 'the class of all predicates that cannot be predicated of themselves', where any predicate may be used to determine a class. The axiom that formalizes this idea is known as the 'comprehension axiom' of naïve set theory. To avoid the reference to classes such as 'the class of all classes that are not members of themselves' Russell restricts this axiom by means of the rules of grammar and the semantics of the type theory. All sentences are arranged into a hierarchy (sentences about individuals at the lowest level, sentences about classes of individuals at the next lowest level, sentences about classes of classes of individuals at the next lowest level and so on). The vicious circle principle, borrowed from Poincaré, states that all definitions should be non-circular, that is, predicative. According to his solution, the propositional function 'x is a class' may not be applied to itself, that is, in Russell's perfect language all objects for which a given predicate holds must be of the same type.

Logicism requires that ordinary language be replaced by a logically perfect language which truly captures logical form. This view also motivated Russell's theory of descriptions (On Denoting, 1905). The true logical form of description sentences such as 'The present King of France is bald' has to be unmasked by showing how the grammatical (subject–predicate) structure translates into a kind of existential sentence in which the apparently denoting phrase 'The present King of France' does not occur. This theory made it possible to avoid positing non-existing entities as the semantic values of fictional names; it was therefore useful for his ontology. It also served his epistemology which required that every constituent of immediate objects of thought and experience be something with which we are directly acquainted. It was also crucial for his logicism. [NBG]

Saccheri, Girolamo. Girolamo Saccheri (1667–1733) was an Italian logician and Jesuit priest, best known for his inadvertent anticipation of non-Euclidean geometry. His textbook, *Logica Demonstrativa* (1697: Pavia), makes extensive use of the inference rule of *consequentia mirabilis*, $(\neg\varphi \to \varphi) \to \varphi$, that any proposition that follows from its own negation must be true. This seemingly paradoxical rule may be traced back to Aristotle, but for Saccheri it was a distinctive feature of fundamental truths that they could be proved no other way.

In *Euclides ab Omni Nævo Vindicatus* (1733, Milan) Saccheri sought to 'clear Euclid of every flaw' through application of his favourite inference. Since antiquity, Euclid's chief flaw was held to be the axiomatic status of the parallel postulate, which states that if two straight lines cut a third, making acute interior angles on the same side, they must ultimately meet, if projected far enough. This was seen as less intuitive than the other axioms, and numerous attempts were made to derive it from them. Saccheri sought to derive the parallel postulate from its own negation (and the other axioms), thereby showing that the postulate must be true. This innovative approach had an unexpected result: the first articulation of non-Euclidean geometry.

Figure 12 Saccheri quadrilateral.

Saccheri constructed a quadrilateral with two opposite sides of equal length, both perpendicular to one of the other sides. He showed that the remaining two angles must be equal, and that they are right angles if and only if the parallel postulate obtains. Otherwise, the angles must be obtuse or acute: Saccheri claimed to derive the parallel postulate from both hypotheses. However, in the acute case the derivation is invalid: Saccheri's results may be understood retrospectively as elementary hyperbolic geometry. Moreover, elliptic geometry may be derived from the obtuse case by foregoing another of Euclid's postulates, the indefinite extensibility of lines. [AA]

Skolem, Thoralf. Thoralf Skolem (1887–1963) simplified Löwenheim's theorem which states that if a first-order theory requires models of infinite size, models can be constructed of any infinite size. 'Skolem's paradox' refers to the observation that first-order theories which yield theorems asserting the existence of uncountably many (or more) objects have denumerable models. [RM]

Stoics. The main representatives of Greek Stoicism are Zeno of Citium (344–262 BC), Cleanthes (d. 232 BC) and Chrysippus (d. 206 BC). Only fragments of their works are known, and Chrysippus is the main source for understanding the importance of the Stoic physics and logic. The only complete works are from the Roman Stoics, that is, Seneca (4 BC–65 AD), Epictetus (55–135) and Marcus Aurelius (121–180), and mainly focus on ethical questions.

The Stoic logic (*logikê*) describes the functions of discourse (*logos*), and involves a study of argument forms, rhetoric, grammar, predicates, propositions, perceptions and thought. It defines the three following entities: signification, signifier and referent. While a signifier (utterance) and a referent (object in the world) are physical, a signification is incorporeal and amounts to what is 'sayable' (*lekton*). Predicates are incomplete *lekta*, and propositions are complete *lekta*, meaning that only propositions are either true or false. Propositions and predicates are rational contents of thought, and the validity of a rational argument follows five logical rules (called indemonstrable forms), namely:

(1) If there is *p*, then there is *q*. There is *p*. Therefore, there is *q* (*modus ponens*).
(2) If there is *p*, then there is *q*. There is no *q*. Therefore, there is no *p* (*modus tollens*).
(3) It is not the case that there are both *p* and *q*. There is *p*. Therefore, there is no *q*.
(4) There is either *p* or *q*. There is *p*. Therefore, there is no *q*.
(5) There is either *p* or *q*. There is no *p*. Therefore, there is *q*.

Bivalence and the law of excluded middle apply even to statements about future states of affairs. Unlike Aristotle, the Stoics reject the contingency of the future, because of their belief in causal determinism, asserting that everything happens through antecedent causes. The justification lies in Stoic physics, in which God (understood as creative fire) includes within itself all physical events, whether past, present or future. Therefore, all things happen through physical fate, in such a way that a present state of affairs causally determines a future one.

The Stoics also tell us that the criterion of truth is provided by cognitive impression, which amounts to the perception of a particular object from which an incorporeal or abstract signification is generated, that is, what is 'sayable' (also called proposition or complete *lekton*). Perception and thinking are necessarily connected, in the sense that the content of a proposition always originates from a given perception. Yet, cognitive impressions do not constitute knowledge, as they merely grasp some individual facts. Only the assent to a cognitive impression will produce knowledge. While a weak assent is a belief (*doxa*) involving an act of ignorance, a strong assent is knowledge (*epistêmê*) and cannot be mistaken. Knowledge means that the cognitive impressions are secure, firm and unchangeable; and only the wise are able to reach knowledge. [JLH]

Tarski, Alfred. Alfred Tarski (1901–1983) was a logician and mathematician of the highest order. Born in Poland, he studied and later worked there until 1939. While on a visit to America in that year World War II broke out, and Tarski was forced to remain in the America, and he remained there for the rest of his life. It is not possible to cover all of Tarski's many achievements here, and so I will concentrate on that for which he is most famous: his definition of truth in formal languages.

It is generally agreed that Tarski's work on truth is important, but precisely why is hotly disputed. Tarski's own view was that unless a precise definition of truth could be given, many important logical results that made use of the semantic notion of truth would remain unclear and strictly unproven (e.g. Gödel's completeness theorem). So, at the very least, we can see Tarski as laying down a foundation for formal semantics in the same way as the logicists were attempting to lay down a foundation for mathematics. Whether his work has any implications for the philosophical question 'what is truth?' is unclear, and Tarski himself claimed that he did not understand this philosophical question anyway (see, e.g., his seminal 'The Semantic Conception of Truth and the Foundations of Semantics' §14).

Two particularly influential elements of Tarski's formal definition of truth are: (i) that it was constructed in order to satisfy what Tarski called 'the material adequacy condition', and (ii) it avoids the liar paradox.

The Material Adequacy Condition. Consider the following form of sentence (where 'p' is a sentence-variable and 'X' a name for that sentence):

(T) X is true if and only if p.
[Example: 'Snow is white' is true if and only if snow is white.]

Tarski recognized that the acceptance of such biconditionals forms a very basic part of our concept of truth. However, as any language containing sentential connectives such as 'and' will contain an infinite number of sentences, he realized that we cannot give an adequate definition of truth merely by conjoining all such biconditionals, so instead Tarski laid it down as a necessary condition that any tenable definition of truth must entail all sentences of this form. And his definition did just that.

The Liar Paradox. Tarski made a distinction between the language for which we want to define truth (the 'object language') and the language in which we actually give the definition (the 'metalanguage') in order to avoid the liar paradox, which can be appreciated most easily by considering the following sentence:

This sentence is false.

Without Tarski's distinction this sentence leads to contradiction: if it is supposed to be true, it has to be false, and if it is supposed to be false, it has to be true. Any definition of truth that leads to contradiction is, at the very least, *prima facie* objectionable. The distinction Tarski gives avoids it because, according to it, the concept of truth expressed in a language cannot apply to any sentences within that language, so sentences of the above form simply cannot be expressed. [BC]

Turing, Alan. British mathematician and logician (1912–1954) who pioneered computability theory, cryptanalysis, computer science and artificial intelligence.

In 1936 Turing solved in the negative the decision problem. The classical formulation of the decision problem is provided by Hilbert and Ackermann in their *Grundzüge der theoretischen Logik* (1928): is it possible to find a procedure that allows one to decide whether a mathematical expression is valid? Turing's first step was to work out a precise definition of the apparently self-evident notion of 'procedure'. He invented an abstract machine, now called Turing machine, which can read and write the cells of an infinite tape, using only two symbols, 0 and 1; the machine performs operations according to a table of rules that specifies, for every state, the corresponding action. Turing proposed to identify the set of the functions calculable by a procedure with the set of the functions calculable by Turing machines. With the help of a diagonal argument similar to those employed by Cantor and Gödel, using the fact that Turing machines can be ordered, Turing showed how to effectively define a real number that is not computable by any Turing machine. Thus he proved that some perfectly defined mathematical problems are not solvable by means of a procedure or an effective method.

Turing proved the existence of a universal Turing machine, that is a machine that can compute, by means of a suitable set of instructions, every function calculable by every other Turing machine. The universal Turing machine is the theoretical prototype of modern computers. After the World War II,

Turing tried to turn the abstract universal Turing machine in a physical reality, and took part in projects for building electronic computers. He designed both the Automatic Computing Engine (ACE), and the programming system of Mark I, which is usually regarded as the second commercially available electronic computer.

In 1950 Turing introduced the 'imitation game' as means of answering the question 'Can machines think?' The game is played with three people, a man (A), a woman (B), and an interrogator who may be of either sex. The interrogator stays in a room apart from the other two players and communicates with them with a teleprinter; he (or she) can ask any sort of question to the other two. The object of the game for the interrogator is to determine which of the other two is the man and which is the woman. A's goal is to deceive the interrogator, whereas B's is to help the interrogator. In a second version of the game a computer takes the part of A. The computer is considered intelligent if it deceives the interrogator in the same proportion in which A deceives the interrogator in the first version of the game. In order to attain its goal, the computer is allowed to lie (e.g., to the question 'Are you the computer?' it can answer 'No, I'm the human being'). The imitation game avoids hard questions about consciousness: if the computer acts like an intelligent human being then it is deemed to be truly intelligent. [MMu]

Venn, John. British logician and historian of logic (1834–1923) who coined the term 'Symbolic logic' and invented the well-known logic diagrams that bear his name. He published an influential logic trilogy: *The Logic of Chance* (1866, 3rd edn, 1888), *Symbolic Logic* (1881, 2nd edn, 1894) and *The Principles of Empirical or Inductive Logic* (1889, 2nd edn, 1907). He is also remembered as a pioneer of the frequency interpretation of probability and as a strong champion of Boole's logic which he defended against Jevons' criticism. [AM]

Whitehead, Alfred North. Whitehead (1861–1947) was a British mathematician and philosopher. His academic career is divided into three stages, during each of which he made important contributions to separate areas within philosophy: 1885–1910, mathematics and logic; 1910–1924, philosophy of science; 1924–1947, metaphysics. Given the scope of this volume, we will focus predominantly on the first stage here.

Whitehead was appointed lecturer in mathematics at Trinity College, Cambridge, in 1885 where he was to remain for the next 25 years. Initially he focussed mainly on teaching and published very little. But in 1891, apparently due to the influence of his wife, he became more productive and started work on his *Treatise on Universal Algebra*, the publication of which in 1898 resulted in Whitehead's election to the Royal Society. During this period Bertrand Russell entered Cambridge as an undergraduate. Recognizing Russell's brilliance, Whitehead secured for him a substantial fellowship and became something of a mentor to him. In around 1900, the two began one of the most celebrated collaborations within philosophy. Over the next 13 years they worked together to produce the seminal three-volume *Principia Mathematica* (1910, 1912, 1913). The book, which is an in-depth defence of logicism conducted in light of the set-theoretical paradoxes discovered by Russell in 1901, has been massively influential, and is considered by many to be one of the greatest intellectual achievements of mankind.

Whitehead's later work in the philosophy of science and metaphysics, conducted at Imperial College in London and Harvard University respectively, also broke new ground. In the philosophy of science, for example, he presented an alternative view to Einstein's theory of relativity, and in metaphysics he developed the view that we ought to think of the fundamental constituents of reality as being processes rather than substances. [BC]

Wittgenstein, Ludwig. Ludwig Wittgenstein (1889–1951) is widely regarded as one of the most important philosophers of the twentieth century. He had a great influence on analytic philosophy. His early philosophy influenced logical positivism; his later philosophy the so-called ordinary language school.

Tractatus Logico-Philosophicus was the only philosophical book Wittgenstein published during his life time. However, he left a large *Nachlass* or unpublished works (published on CD-ROM in 2000), including his masterwork *Philosophical Investigations* (published in 1953).

In the *Tractatus*, Wittgenstein held that every proposition is a truth-functional combination of elementary propositions. Elementary propositions are contingent and mutually logically independent. So their truth-functional combinations must be contingent propositions, tautologies and contradictions. All (true) logical propositions are tautologies. The rules of logical operation are the constitutive rules of language.

In 1929, Wittgenstein changed his mind on an issue he considered in the *Tractatus*, namely, determinate exclusion. He no longer thought that such a proposition as 'A is red and blue all over' is analysable into one containing a contradiction – his new position was that it is nonsensical. He suggested that logical operations depend on the content of the propositions connected. This undermined the foundations of the *Tractatus*, since it necessitated abandoning the independence of elementary propositions and the view that all necessity is a result of truth-functional combination.

Wittgenstein turned to a radical reconsideration of the *Tractatus* conceptions of language and logic. His mature reflections on this are in the *Philosophical Investigations*. He still held that language is a rule-governed activity, but the concepts of language and rule are now taken to be family resemblance concepts. There is no common essence of language. Rather, there is a multiplicity of language-games connected by overlapping similarities. The meaning of an expression is what we understand when we understand the expression, and can be given by an explanation. An explanation of meaning provides a rule for the correct use of the expression. For a large class of cases, the meaning of an expression is its use. Understanding an expression is akin to an ability. When we are able to follow the rule governing the use of an expression, we understand it. Following a rule, and thus understanding, consists in the actual practice of acting in accordance with the rule. Logic still has an intimate relation to language. But, unlike the calculus view of logic as the constitutive rules of language in the *Tractatus*, logic only gives rules for the transformation of symbols and not all the rules of grammar, where 'grammar' refers to the constitutive rules of language-games.

In the *Philosophical Investigations*, with his grammatical investigations of meaning and rule-following, Wittgenstein sought to overthrow the pervading empiricist and rationalist conceptions of the mind and of self-consciousness. This includes his demonstrations of the impossibility of private language.

Wittgenstein wrote extensively on the philosophy of mathematics. In the *Tractatus*, numbers are defined in terms of the successive applications of a logical operation. In his later writings, he rejected both the realist conception of numbers as objects and the formalist identification of numbers with numerals. The meaning of a numeral is determined by the rule of its use. In general, mathematics is seen as a system of rules for the transformation of propositions concerning magnitudes.

Wittgenstein also appeared to identify truth in a calculus with provability, and to dismiss Gödel's incompleteness theorem by arguing that propositions like 'P is true and unprovable (in *Principia Mathematica*)' are nonsensical. Earlier commentators thought that Wittgenstein failed to understand Gödel's proof, especially the syntactic notion of truth and the consistency assumption. Recently, however, some commentators have offered new and more sympathetic interpretations of Wittgenstein's view on Gödel's theorem. [LC]

Key Texts: Textbooks

Beginning Logic (1965), **E.J. Lemmon.** Lemmon's well-regarded book is a classic introductory textbook on propositional logic and predicate logic. There is a strong emphasis on proof using natural deduction. Truth table construction for propositional logic and a little elementary meta-logic are also included. [SML]

From Frege to Gödel (1967), **J. van Heijenoort.** This is probably the most influential book in the historiography of logic. It established the view that Gottlob Frege was the father of modern logic. The book reproduces chronologically 46 key texts in the development of mathematical logic, opening with Frege's *Begriffsschrift* (1879) and concluding with Herbrand's response to Gödel (1931). Each text is introduced and many were translated for the first time into English. In spite of several serious omissions, it is still today the standard source book in mathematical logic. [AM]

Introduction to Logic (1953), **I.M. Copi and C. Cohen.** First published in 1953, this book has become the most widely used introductory textbook to logic, and is now in its 13th edition. The current edition retains the basic three-part structure of the original: (1) The basic concepts of logic are introduced via a wealth of real-life examples of arguments (both good and bad) from everyday life. (2) Deductive reasoning and modern symbolic logic are developed. (3) Finally, inductive reasoning is covered with sections relating the methods described directly to science and the theory of probability. [BC]

Logic (2005), **L. Goldstein, A. Brennan, M. Deutsch and J.Y.F. Lau.** A gentle, sometimes humorous, introduction to logic and surrounding philosophical issues. It discusses topics including truth, proof, entailment, reference, vagueness, the nature of logic and some objections to logic, for example that it is anti-women and anti-God. It is published in English, Portuguese, Spanish. [LG]

Logic (1977), **W. Hodges.** This introductory textbook focuses on the logic of truth-functional connectives, quantifiers and relations and uses semantic trees. Though formal logic is covered, natural language is at the forefront of the approach. Insights and devices from linguistics (including phrase-markers) are used. [SML]

Logic with Trees (1997), **C. Howson.** This textbook in logic and meta-logic uses semantic trees and includes coverage of the method of proof by induction and of soundness and completeness results for propositional logic and predicate logic. The last chapter covers conditionals and modality. [SML]

Logic: Techniques of Formal Reasoning (1964), **D. Kalish and R. Montague.** This is a student text on first-order logic, distinctive for using direct proof procedures, and for employing complete terms for definite descriptions. In the latter respect it follows Frege, except that in the case of improper definite descriptions their designation is chosen to be the number 0. It was updated by Kalish and Mar in 1980, and then included a discussion of several 'Russellian' Theories of Descriptions. [HS]

Naive Set Theory (1960), **P. Halmos.** This is an informal but rigorous description of standard set theory. Paul Halmos was an accomplished American mathematician famous for writing in informative, lucid prose. 'Naïve' in the title refers to the conversational, non-axiomatic style of the book, written 'perched on the end of a bed' while on holiday. [ZW]

The Logic of Real Arguments (1988), **A. Fisher.** A contribution to the critical thinking literature, Fisher's book gives thorough analyses of serious arguments (Malthus, Marx, Mill), not everyday discourse, provides a method of identifying arguments and their implicit assumptions ('what would justify the conclusion?'), and offers an account of suppositional reasoning that is applied to conditionals. [EB]

Key Texts: Classics

A System of Logic (1843), **J. S. Mill.** John Stuart Mill's *A System of Logic, Ratiocinative and Inductive: Being a Connected View of the Principles of Evidence and the Methods of Scientific Investigation* (1843. 7th edition. London: Longmans, Green, Reader and Dyer) displays, in book one, an analysis of language. It restores the medieval distinction between denotation and connotation, and states that names denote things rather than ideas, a theory later much disparaged by Frege for neglecting the descriptive content of words.

The *System of Logic* then puts forward a theory of deductive reasoning in book two, based on associationalism, Mill's psychological doctrine. Books five and six address the fallacies and the logic of the moral sciences respectively. But its originality mostly lies in books three and four, which defend an empirical approach to mathematics and logics: no proposition being known a priori, all knowledge has grounds in natural facts.

At the heart of the *System* lies the theory of induction, which is the operation of discovering and proving general propositions. A general proposition is a mere juxtaposition of particular cases. Therefore, reasoning is always an inference from particulars to particulars. Why is it legitimate to generalize from samples? The grounds of induction is the axiom of the uniformity of the course of nature. It is the implicit major premise of all syllogisms from which scientific laws are deduced. Thus, Mill's theory of induction also provides a justification for deduction, which is most fundamental in his eyes.

Mill developed a canon of scientific reasoning, within which he conceived inductive reasoning to be tantamount to Aristotle's theory of syllogism for deduction. Mill's Canon is composed of four methods of experimental inquiry (agreement, difference, residues and concomitant variations), which aim to identify the cause of a given phenomenon. [JMC]

***Begriffsschrift (1879)*, G. Frege.** *Begriffsschrift* is the book that inaugurated modern logic. Written by the German mathematician Gottlob Frege and published in 1879, it gave the first exposition of predicate logic, introducing a notation for quantification, and also offered an axiomatization of propositional logic. The book is divided into three parts. The first part explains Frege's logical symbolism, which he called 'Begriffsschrift' (literally, 'concept-script'), the second shows how to represent and derive certain propositions and the third uses the symbolism to provide a logical analysis of mathematical induction.

Frege's crucial innovation lay in extending the use of function-argument analysis from mathematics to logic. In traditional (Aristotelian) logic, simple propositions such as 'Gottlob is cool' had been seen as having subject–predicate form, represented by '*S* is *P*', with '*S*' symbolizing the subject and '*P*' the predicate, joined together by the copula 'is'. In Fregean logic, they are seen as having function-argument form, represented by '*Fa*', with '*a*' symbolizing the argument (in this case Gottlob) and '*x* is *F*' the function (in this case, the concept *is cool*), the '*x*' here indicating where the argument term goes to yield the proposition.

With a notation for quantification, more complex propositions such as 'All logicians are cool' (involving the quantifier 'All') can then be formalized. Traditional logic had also seen these as having subject–predicate form, 'All logicians' in this case being the subject. In Fregean logic, however, this is seen as having a quite different and more complex (quantificational) form: in modern notation, symbolized as '$(\forall x)\,(Lx \rightarrow Cx)$', that is, 'For all *x*, if *x* is a logician, then *x* is cool'. The advantages of Fregean logic come out, especially, when we consider statements of multiple generality (involving more than one quantifier), such as 'Every philosopher loves some logician', which traditional logic had great difficulty in analysing. [MB]

***Computability and Logic (1974),* G.S. Boolos and R. Jeffrey.** A textbook in classical computability theory and logic written by George Stephen Boolos (1940–1996) and Richard Jeffrey (1926–2002) and first published by Cambridge University Press (CUP) in 1974. This esteemed book received its reputation because it is highly readable and pedagogical. The book assumes a minimal mathematical background – some familiarity with propositional calculus. In fact, even readers with no prior knowledge of propositional calculus can easily read the book as there is a chapter that presents the relevant ideas. The book has three parts – the first part is about computability theory, the second part introduces basic as well as advanced topics in symbolic logic and in the third part there is a discussion of more specialized topics. In particular, in the first part of the book there is a thorough discussion of Turing machines and Turing computability, abacus computability (i.e. an alternative but equivalent formulation of Turing computability), recursion theory and a presentation of the Church-Turing thesis, which is correctly characterized as a hypothesis. Interestingly enough in the second chapter, the authors introduce the Zeus character to explain enumerable sets and, thus, implicitly introduce the notion of a *supertask* (i.e. an infinite process that completes in finite time). The second part starts with a refresher of first-order logic and goes on to discuss models, proof theory, arithmetization (i.e. Gödel numbers) and Gödel's incompleteness theorems. The third part of the book presents some special topics in proof theory and logic. Last, but certainly not least, the exercises at the end of each chapter have been designed to help students easily grasp topics that are introduced in later chapters. [AS]

Laws of Thought (1854), **G. Boole.** Boole assumed that human thought processes could be expressed in terms of logical operations. In Boole's most important mathematical work, *An Investigation of the Laws of Thought on which are FOUNDED the Mathematical Theories of Logic and Probabilities* (1854. London: Macmillan and Co.), he starts by saying 'The design of the following treatise is to investigate the fundamental laws of those operations of the mind by which reasoning is performed . . . ' In other words, he intended to develop the laws required in order to express human logic mathematically. To this end, Boole developed an algebra to determine the validity of propositions, in which 0 represented FALSE and 1 represented TRUE. These laws, which govern the relationships between true / false statements in logic, comprised the first steps to what we now call Boolean logic (algebra).

Boolean algebra contains the additional logical operations AND, OR and NOT and includes the corresponding set-theoretic operations intersection, union and complement. For example, consider the proposition 'I will cycle to work if it is sunny and it is not windy.' With C for CYCLE, S for SUNNY, W for WINDY we write the proposition as a Boolean equation:

C=S AND not-W which states that C is true iff S is true and not-W is true and which constitutes a logical representation of our original sentence.

Boolean algebra subsequently provided the basis for much of computer science; Claude Shannon working at MIT in the 1940s developed the mathematics of binary information processing, based on Boole's work. [DH]

Logical Foundations of Probability (1950), **R. Carnap.** This book presents Carnap's views on confirmation, induction and the concepts of logical and frequentist probability. Its central tenets are that all inductive inference is probabilistic, that the required concept of probability derives from logical relations between evidence and hypotheses, and that inductive inferences are therefore analytic. The book laid the groundwork for quantitative inductive logic in the second half of the twentieth century.

The book starts with a description of the problem, and of Carnap's philosophical methodology of concept explication. Then two distinct notions of probability are introduced, logical probability pertaining to confirmation, and factual probability pertaining to long-run relative frequency. Subsequently the language systems of deductive logic are introduced to furnish inductive logical systems, and a general characterization of the problem of inductive logic is given. This leads to the development of regular c-functions, which express the confirmation of hypotheses by evidence as a partial entailment, in analogy to deductive entailment, and the measure r, which expresses relevance relations between evidence and hypotheses. The functions c and r are shown to capture a pre-theoretical notion of comparative and qualitative confirmation. The book then deals with the class of symmetric c-functions, which are invariant under permutations of terms in the language. Finally, c-functions are shown to perform the same function as estimators in classical statistics. An appendix introduces to the confirmation function c^*, which forms the basis for much of the later work in inductive logic.

Carnap wrote a separate treatise on quantitative inductive systems like c^* (Carnap, R. 1952. *The Continuum of Inductive Methods*. Chicago: University of Chicago Press). An influential but contentious criticism of Carnap's programme was mounted by Goodman (Goodman, N. 1955. *Fact, Fiction, and Forecast*. Cambridge MA: Harvard UP). An overview of the inductive logic initiated by Carnap is *Studies in Inductive Logic and Probability* Vol 1 (1980. Carnap, R. and Jeffrey, R.C. [eds] Berkeley: University of California Press). [JWR]

Logique de Port-Royal (1662), A. Arnauld and P. Nicole. The *Port-Royal Logic* is the popular name for Antoine Arnauld and Pierre Nicole's *La Logique, ou l'Art de Penser*, the most influential logic text between the seventeenth and nineteenth centuries. The nickname is derived from the convent of Port-Royal, near Paris, with which both men were associated. According to the authors, the *Logic* was originally composed by Arnauld to make good on a boast that he could teach a teenage nobleman, Charles-Honoré d'Albert, subsequently Duke of Chevreuse, all that was worth knowing about logic in no more than five days. After this work had begun to circulate in manuscript, Arnauld collaborated with Nicole to prepare a version for publication. During the authors' lifetimes, the work was published in five editions, between 1662 and 1683. It was first translated into English in 1674, and most recently and faithfully by Jill Vance Buroker (1996. Cambridge: Cambridge University Press).

The *Logic* is divided into four parts, covering ideas, propositions, reasoning and method, respectively. The second and third parts comprise a conventional, if engagingly written, summary of the scholastic logic of categorical propositions and syllogisms. Throughout, the authors emphasize the practical application of logic in the evaluation and composition of reasoning, and disarmingly dismiss much of the theory they summarize as of use only for exercising the mind. However, unlike some seventeenth-century critics of scholasticism, they demonstrate a sophisticated grasp of its key tenets. The other two parts are more original, and display the influence of René Descartes and Arnauld and Nicole's fellow Jansenist Blaise Pascal.

Part one recapitulates Descartes's argument that intellectual intuition can be a source of 'clear and distinct ideas', which are thereby self-evident. This is understood as providing justification for absolute truths in both science and religion. Part four also echoes Descartes, with an account of scientific method which stresses the mathematical over the empirical and downplays the long-standing distinction between synthesis, or working forward from the premises to the conclusion, and analysis, or working backward from the conclusion to the premises. Arnauld and Nicole's impatience with empiricism, rhetoric and especially Michel de Montaigne's scepticism with respect to the efficacy of reason are also characteristically Cartesian. The influence of Pascal is evident in the account of definition, which clarifies the ultimately Aristotelean distinction between nominal and real definitions as specifying respectively how the word is used, and how the idea for which it stands is related to other ideas. Arnauld and Nicole also helped to fix the now standard distinction between extension and intension as distinguishing the individuals to which a term refers from the ideas which it represents.

The *Port-Royal Logic* was the principal conduit by which the Cartesian approach to logic was transmitted. This influence was perhaps greatest in the context of theological epistemology: the *Logic* found favour with Protestant as well as Catholic colleges, and influenced later religious-minded logicians, such as Isaac Watts. Latterly, the humanistic emphasis of the work has been praised as anticipating argumentation theory – see Maurice Finnochiaro (1997. The Port-Royal Logic's theory of argument. *Argumentation*, 11: 393–410). [AA]

Mathematical Logic (1940), W. Quine. First published in 1940, this book was based upon Quine's graduate teaching during the 1930s at Harvard University. He presents a new system of mathematical logic that he claimed was accessible to those with no previous exposure to formal logic. But it was supposed to serve not just as an introduction to the subject, but also as a serious contribution to logic – or as Quine puts it in the preface: as a 'textbook and treatise . . . within the same covers'. The serious contribution the book was intended to make was in the vein of logicism, that is, to show that mathematics is reducible to logic. The system Quine outlines in the book was supposed to avoid the known set-theoretical paradoxes in a simpler and more satisfying way than any proposed by previous authors, and in particular Russell and Whitehead in *Principia Mathematica*. With one caveat, this claim is considered to be substantiated. The caveat is that the system presented in the first edition of *Mathematical Logic* was discovered by Barkley Rosser to be inconsistent (specifically, a paradox called the Burali-Forti paradox could be derived from it), but this mistake was rectified in the second edition.

Chapter 1 is an elegant account of the propositional calculus. Chapter 2 introduces quantification theory. In chapters 3 and 4 Quine applies the general theory to the study of classes, and it is these two chapters that contain the core of Quine's new system. In chapter 5 Quine shows us how to reduce relations to classes. In Chapter 6 we are given the derivation of mathematics from logic, where the numbers (natural, rational and real) and arithmetical operations are again defined in terms of classes. Finally, in chapter 7 we are given a sharply delineated proof of an incompleteness theorem that closely parallels Gödel's famous result. [BC]

Novum Organum (1620), **F. Bacon.** The *Novum Organum* (Bacon, F.
1620/1994. Trans. and ed. Urbach, P. and Gibson, J. Chicago: Open Court) is
the principal philosophical work of Sir Francis Bacon, the English scholar and
statesman. It contains his pioneering account of scientific method. The title
stakes a bold claim: that this account should supersede Aristotle's *Organon*,
the dominant theory of logic for two millennia. The *Novum Organum*
comprises the incomplete second part of a projected six-part Latin work, the
Instauratio Magna, a proposed 'Great Reconstruction' of human knowledge.
The first part translated his earlier vernacular work *The Advancement of
Learning* (Bacon, F. 1605/1915. London: J. M. Dent & Sons), but the later
parts dealing with specific sciences were never finished.

The two completed books of the *Novum Organum* offer guidance on the
avoidance of past error and the establishment of new knowledge, respectively. In the most influential passage from the first part, Bacon distinguished
four important sources of error in received ideas, which he described as
'Idols'. The 'Idols of the Tribe' are subjective opinions so widespread among
humanity that we accept them as necessary; the 'Idols of the Cave' are
individual prejudices which we fail to recognize: the cave represents the
self by allusion to Plato's Myth of the Cave; the 'Idols of the Marketplace'
are errors that result from the imprecision of language· words acquire their
meanings from vulgar exchange; the 'Idols of the Theatre' are the tenets of
prevailing philosophical or scientific theories, which come and go like actors
on the stage.

Part two begins the exposition of Bacon's account of scientific method. Bacon
first explores an example, an inquiry into the nature of heat. Bacon recommends the compilation of three tables: first, of 'Existence and Presence', a list
of circumstances in which the phenomenon occurs, made as diverse as possible; secondly of 'Deviation, or Absence in Proximity', which seeks to correlate
each of the entries in the first table with similar circumstances in which the
phenomenon is not found; lastly of 'Degrees' or 'Comparison', which itemises
cases where the phenomenon may occur to a greater or lesser degree. From
these three tables Bacon is able to compile a further table, of 'Exclusion or
Rejection of Natures', which uses the accumulated data to rule out explanations inconsistent with that data. Once this has been attempted, Bacon
recommends proceeding to a 'First Vintage': a draft explanation of the
phenomenon.

The novelty of Bacon's method lies in the systematic and thorough appraisal of evidence behind the First Vintage. Nonetheless, overemphasis on its significance lies behind the widespread interpretation of Bacon as advocating a mechanical procedure for extracting watertight theories from pretheoretic observation. Although Bacon's name has become strongly linked to this naive inductivist position, more accurate readings stress that the First Vintage is itself subject to revision in the light of further data.

The remainder of Part two addresses 27 'Prerogative Instances'. This is Bacon's term for different circumstances in which empirical data can become manifest. Notable examples include 'Shining Instances', evidence which provides overwhelming prima facie support for a specific theory, and 'Crucial Instances', or 'Instances of the Fingerpost', experiments whose outcome promises to settle disputes between competing theories. [AA]

***Organon (4th Century BC)*, Aristotle.** The *Organon* ('instrument' or 'tool') is the name given by Aristotle's followers to his six works on logic: *Categories, De Interpretatione, Prior Analytics, Posterior Analytics, Topics* and *Sophistical Refutations*. The order of the works is not chronological but forms a well-structured collection.

The *Categories* deals with the classification of all existing things, which are the substance and the nine accidents (i.e. quantity, quality, relation, place, time, position, having, acting and being acted upon).

The *De Interpretatione* introduces the concepts of sentence (*logos*) and belief (*doxa*). A sentence is a significant spoken sound, uttered at a given time. The contradictory of a true sentence is always false, when the subject of that sentence is a universal ('every man' or 'no man') or a particular ('Socrates' or 'some man'). By contrast, when a universal is not spoken of universally ('a man'), it is then true to say at the same time that, say, 'a man is pale' and 'a man is not pale'. Moreover, future-tensed sentences are neither true nor false: they are contingent, owing to the impossibility of knowing the future (e.g. a future sea battle may or may not occur).

The *Prior Analytics* examines the notion of syllogism, which is a three-term argument (with two premisses and a conclusion) understood as a deductive inference. The well-known instance is: All men are mortal (major premise); Socrates is a man (minor premise); therefore, Socrates is mortal. The truth of the two premisses makes the conclusion true.

The *Posterior Analytics* is interested in science or knowledge (*epistêmê*): it shows how general reasoning can be said to be correct through the different forms of syllogism. A demonstration is a deduction (or perfect syllogism), in which the true premisses are primary, immediate, better known than, prior to and explanatory of the conclusion. On the other hand, induction is analysed as the argument from a particular to a universal: it explains the way we know the indemonstrable first principles of sciences.

The *Topics* introduces the art of dialectic: it is the method for discovering a set of beliefs, playing the role of premisses in a syllogistic argument. The aim is to determine which premisses an interlocutor is ready to accept. Aristotle also suggests a classification of arguments based on opposites (contraries, contradictions, possession/privation and relatives), cases (nominative, accusative, etc.) and probable inferences (using the terms 'more', 'less' and 'likewise').

The *Sophistical Refutations*, in connection with Aristotle's work on rhetoric, studies a series of logical fallacies. Some syllogisms are only apparent, when the conclusion does not genuinely follow from the premisses; likewise, it is possible for some acceptable syllogisms to have unacceptable premisses.

Note that many views developed in the *Organon* would no longer be regarded as belonging to logic nowadays. On the other hand, Aristotle's *Metaphysics*, which is not included in the *Organon*, deals with genuine logical problems, for example, the principle of non-contradiction. [JLH]

***Principia Mathematica (1910–1913)*, A. N. Whitehead and B. Russell.**
One of the most important intellectual achievements of the last century, the
Principia is an epic attempt to demonstrate that logic underlies mathematics.
The work is at least as important for its symbolic value as its actual content:
it is a monument of logic.

Frege argued for logicism: the thesis that mathematical truth is reducible to
logical truth. Early in his career, Russell came to agree with Frege, and wrote
The Principles of Mathematics in 1905, which argued for logicism in informal
prose. Alfred North Whitehead had reached similar conclusions and at the
same time. To vindicate the logicist programme, though, someone would
eventually need to do the hard work of starting from primitive logical assumptions, and reasoning step by step with no gaps up to the basic theorems of
set theory, arithmetic, analysis (calculus) and geometry. Between 1910 and
1913, Russell and Whitehead produced the *Principia*, which purports to do
just that.

Frege himself had attempted such a feat in his own 'concept notation', but
the system turned out, quite surprisingly, to be trivial – in it one could have
proved anything at all. The *Principia*, therefore, was preoccupied with avoid-
ing the paradoxes of Frege's system, and to this end in a long but accessible
introduction, Russell explains his solutions: the vicious circle principle (VCP)
and type theory. The VCP says that 'whatever involves all of a collection
must not be one of that collection'. This bans, among other things, any kind
of self-reference. The theory of types is a technical structure to support
mathematics built to the specifications of the VCP.

Because the theory of types is a complex and demanding system, it has not
been widely adopted. The main body of the *Principia*, too, is an uncomprom-
ising procession of logical formulae, unusual at the time and still today
requiring patience to read. A proof that $1 + 1 = 2$ does not appear until
several hundred pages into the first volume. Above all, the *Principia* fell short
of its goals, because a few non-logical assumptions – the axioms of infinity
and reducibility – were required for the proofs, and most doubt that these
are parts of pure logic. So the complete reduction of mathematics to logic
faltered.

In the end, Whitehead and Russell contributed their own money to publish
the three volumes of *Principia*. Russell wrote of having bad dreams in which

the books lay, dusty and unread, on forgotten library shelves, and spoke afterward of the irreparable mental toll its writing had exacted on him.

Nevertheless, the *Principia* was epochal, the meticulous proofs an inspiration and confirmation that informal mathematical practice could, if we wanted, be exactly translated into formal symbolism and carried out with absolute precision. The book made an indelible impression on philosophers such as Wittgenstein and Quine. And perhaps most importantly, the *Principia* was the system in which Gödel carried out his 1931 incompleteness proofs. For a most important era, the *Principia* was exactly what Russell and Whitehead hoped it would be – a tangible, logical foundation for mathematics. [ZW]

The Development of Logic (1962), W. Kneale and M. Kneale. *The Development of Logic*, by William and Martha Kneale (1962. Oxford: Clarendon Press), traces the development of formal logic from its origin to the present. A historical encyclopaedia of logic, this book does not chronicle all that past scholars, good and bad, have said about logic. Instead, it gives an account of the growth of logic. Consequently, emphasis is put on the authors insofar as they pave the way for modern logic.

The story begins with the Greek philosophers, because the scope of logical studies is determined by the content of Aristotle's *Organon*, and by the Stoics' logic of propositions. Interest in formal logic does not fade away in the medieval period, which is concerned with semantic and inferential issues. In the post-Renaissance period, while logic declines as a branch of philosophy, progress is made in mathematics, and especially in algebra and analysis. When logic is revived in the middle of the nineteenth century, the new vigour comes from mathematicians: geometry provides a field for the working out of the notion of axiomatics, algebra furnishes a model for imitation in the making of a logical calculus. After Boole's mathematical analysis of logic, which exhibits logic as a part of mathematics, the next great advance in logic is made by Frege, whose *Begriffsschrift* (1879), the first really comprehensive system of formal logic, introduces the idea that arithmetic is grounded on logic. Although Frege gives the essentials of modern logic, two developments of the twentieth century make it necessary to reconsider his delimitation of the province of logic: the discovery of the set theory paradoxes and the debate initiated by Wittgenstein about necessity and language. [EC]

Tractatus (1921), L. Wittgenstein. *Tractatus Logico-Philosophicus* was the only philosophical book published by Ludwig Wittgenstein during his lifetime. It aims to draw a limit to thought by determining the limits of its expression in language.

The *Tractatus* ties logic to the nature of linguistic representation. Logical syntax, whose rules distinguish sense from nonsense, is hidden beneath the surface of ordinary language, but recoverable via analysis. A proposition is analysable into a truth-function of elementary propositions. An elementary proposition is a combination of names representing a combination of simple objects.

The *Tractatus* made truth-tables popular. The truth-table presenting an operation, say, disjunction, is:

p	q	p∨q
T	T	T
T	F	T
F	T	T
F	F	F

If the order of the truth-possibilities of 'p' and 'q' in the above schema is fixed conventionally, then the operation can be written as '(TTTF)(p,q)'. In cases with more than two propositions, they can be considered as involving only one operation. For example, the operation in (p∨q)∨r is expressible as '(TTTTTTTF)(p,q,r)'.

The *Tractatus* introduces and defines the operation N in terms of the truth-table as follows: N(ξ̄)=(FF . . . FT)(ξ, . . .), where '(ξ̄)' signifies a collection of the values of the variable ξ which ranges over propositions. If ξ has 'p' as its only value, then N(ξ̄)=(FT)(p)=¬p, and NN(ξ̄)=p. If ξ has two values 'p' and 'q', then N(ξ̄)=(FFFT)(p,q)=~p∧~q, and NN(ξ̄)=p∨q. All logical connectives are definable in terms of negation and disjunction and thus in terms of N. If ξ has as its values all the values of fx, then N(ξ̄)=¬(TT . . . TF)(ξ̄)=¬(∃x)fx, and NN(ξ̄)=(∃x)fx. The existential quantifier and, similarly, the universal quantifier are also definable in terms of N. Consequently, N is the sole fundamental operation of the *Tractatus* formal system.

It has been argued that N is expressively incomplete, because N cannot generate logical equivalents of propositions like '(∃x)(∀y)fxy'. This is not decisive, as Wittgenstein simply does not explain how to specify the scope of N. It has been suggested that N be expressed as 'N(x:fx)', where x specifies the scope. '(∃x)(∀y)(fxy)' can then be rendered as 'N(N(x:N(y:N(fxy))))'.

According to the Church-Turing Theorem, first-order quantification theory with an infinite domain cannot have a decision procedure. But N is defined in terms of the truth-table, and the latter provides a decision procedure. Therefore, N is not well-defined, unless the Tractarian system has only finite sub-domains. Wittgenstein was not aware of such a restriction.

The *Tractatus* accepts the contingency and the logical independence of elementary propositions. This, together with the view that every proposition is a truth-function of them, entails that logical propositions, that is, propositions of logical truth, are truth-functional tautologies. Logical propositions show the nature of the significant propositions which they combine to form tautologies. They, as the limiting cases of significant propositions, constitute the limit of language.

Most of the sentences in the *Tractatus* are elucidations. They, and any utterances about logic, ethics, aesthetics and religion, fall outside the limit of language. Being nonsensical, they neither say nor show anything. Nevertheless, Wittgenstein believed, what they attempt to say is shown by significant propositions. [LC]

Index